# A Student's Guide to

# JACK LONDON

Titles in the **UNDERSTANDING LITERATURE** Series:

A Student's Guide to
## JANE AUSTEN
ISBN-13: 978-0-7660-2439-7
ISBN-10:      0-7660-2439-3

A Student's Guide to
## EMILY DICKINSON
ISBN-13: 978-0-7660-2285-0
ISBN-10:      0-7660-2285-4

A Student's Guide to
## F. SCOTT FITZGERALD
ISBN-13: 978-0-7660-2202-7
ISBN-10:      0-7660-2202-1

A Student's Guide to
## ROBERT FROST
ISBN-13: 978-0-7660-2434-2
ISBN-10:      0-7660-2434-2

A Student's Guide to
## NATHANIEL HAWTHORNE
ISBN-13: 978-0-7660-2283-6
ISBN-10:      0-7660-2283-8

A Student's Guide to
## ERNEST HEMINGWAY
ISBN-13: 978-0-7660-2431-1
ISBN-10:      0-7660-2431-8

A Student's Guide to
## JACK LONDON
ISBN-13: 978-0-7660-2707-7
ISBN-10:      0-7660-2707-4

A Student's Guide to
## HERMAN MELVILLE
ISBN-13: 978-0-7660-2435-9
ISBN-10:      0-7660-2435-0

A Student's Guide to
## ARTHUR MILLER
ISBN-13: 978-0-7660-2432-8
ISBN-10:      0-7660-2432-6

A Student's Guide to
## TONI MORRISON
ISBN-13: 978-0-7660-2436-6
ISBN-10:      0-7660-2436-9

A Student's Guide to
## GEORGE ORWELL
ISBN-13: 978-0-7660-2433-5
ISBN-10:      0-7660-2433-4

A Student's Guide to
## EDGAR ALLAN POE
ISBN-13: 978-0-7660-2437-3
ISBN-10:      0-7660-2437-7

A Student's Guide to
## WILLIAM SHAKESPEARE
ISBN-13: 978-0-7660-2284-3
ISBN-10:      0-7660-2284-6

A Student's Guide to
## JOHN STEINBECK
ISBN-13: 978-0-7660-2259-1
ISBN-10:      0-7660-2259-5

A Student's Guide to
## MARK TWAIN
ISBN-13: 978-0-7660-2438-0
ISBN-10:      0-7660-2438-5

A Student's Guide to
## TENNESSEE WILLIAMS
ISBN-13: 978-0-7660-2706-0
ISBN-10:      0-7660-2706-6

UNDERSTANDING
LITERATURE

# A Student's Guide to

# JACK
# LONDON

## Stephanie Buckwalter

**Enslow Publishers, Inc.**
40 Industrial Road
Box 398
Berkeley Heights, NJ 07922
USA
      http://www.enslow.com

**Library of Congress Cataloging-in-Publication Data**

Buckwalter, Stephanie.
    A student's guide to Jack London / by Stephanie Buckwalter.
        p. cm. — (Understanding literature)
    Includes bibliographical references and index.
    ISBN-13: 978-0-7660-2707-7
    ISBN-10: 0-7660-2707-4
    1. London, Jack, 1876-1916—Criticism and interpretation—Handbooks,
manuals, etc. 2. London, Jack, 1876-1916—Criticism and interpretation—
Juvenile literature. I. Title. II. Series.
    PS3523.O46Z614 2007
    813'.52—dc22
                                      2006032815

Printed in the United States of America

10 9 8 7 6 5 4 3 2 1

**To Our Readers:**
We have done our best to make sure all Internet Addresses in this book were active
and appropriate when we went to press. However, the author and the publisher
have no control over and assume no liability for the material available on those
Internet sites or on other Web sites they may link to. Any comments or suggestions
can be sent by e-mail to comments@enslow.com or to the address on the back
cover.

Every effort has been made to locate all copyright holders of material used
in this book. If any errors or omissions have occurred, corrections will be
made in future editions of this book.

**Illustration Credits:** Bancroft Library, pp. 28, 30; The Granger Collection,
pp. 59, 65; Photo courtesy of Richard Bond and Helen Abbott/The Jack
London Museum, p. 57; Jupiterimages Corporation, pp. 14, 62, 79, 104;
Library of Congress, p. 120; Shutterstock, Inc., pp. 39, 46, 136.

**Cover Illustration:** Library of Congress (inset); Corel Corporation/
Hemera Technologies, Inc./ The Granger Collection (background objects).

# CONTENTS

**1** A Man of the Times
An introduction to the life
and works of Jack London . . . . . . . . . . . . . . . . . . . . .  7

**2** The Making of a Writer
The roots and development of
London's earliest work . . . . . . . . . . . . . . . . . . . . . .  26

**3** The Northland Stories
Examining *The Son of the Wolf*
and other short stories . . . . . . . . . . . . . . . . . . . . . .  42

**4** A Dog Story
Examining *The Call of the Wild* . . . . . . . . . . . . . . . . . .  55

**5** Beyond the Northland
The development of London's socialist views . . . . . .  73

**6** A Love Story
Examining *The Sea-Wolf* . . . . . . . . . . . . . . . . . . . . . .  83

**7** The Other Dog Story
Examining *White Fang* . . . . . . . . . . . . . . . . . . . . . . .  92

**8** The *Snark*
Sea-voyage writings. . . . . . . . . . . . . . . . . . . . . . . . . 102

**9** True-Life Writings
    Revealing the man behind the words............ 113

**10** Farmer and Finale
    The final years and legacy of Jack London ....... 126

Chronology ............................. 141

Chapter Notes........................... 144

Glossary................................. 150

Major Works by Jack London ......... 154

Further Reading ....................... 156

Internet Addresses..................... 157

Index................................... 158

# A Man of the Times

Alfred Kazin once wrote, "The greatest story Jack London ever wrote was the story he lived."[1] Jack London's life story reads like that of the mythical American hero. His rugged individualism and creativity allowed him to live out the rags-to-riches stories he had read as a child. For London, success came early. He was only twenty-seven years old when publication of *The Call of the Wild* catapulted him to international fame.

London constantly sought after adventure and his many exploits provided grist for his writing mill. He had the uncanny ability to capture the essence of an experience and, with a little imagination, turn it into interesting reading. Because of this tendency to romanticize his real-life experiences in his stories, many biographers have taken London's fiction and quoted it as fact. At times, it is hard to tell the difference.

Biographers have another difficulty when faced with London's body of work. As one biographer puts it, "Trying to pinpoint a consistent philosophy in London's work fails."[2] One reason is because London used his writing for many things: to make money, to relive/rewrite his experiences and life story, to promote the socialist cause, and to promote his own philosophies. Another reason is that London was a voracious reader. He sought after the writings of the great thinkers of his day. As he read, he incorporated new ideas into his work. Both his purpose for writing and his philosophy of life were moving targets.

**SOCIALISM**—*An economic system in which the means of production and distribution are owned and operated by the government with all members of society sharing in the work and the products.*

London went through three major life changes. Each time, he added a new dimension to his life's philosophy—or changed it completely. First, his childhood work in the factories and his experience as a hobo gave birth to his identity as a socialist. Second, his trip to the Klondike convinced him that he should be a writer rather than work at manual labor or pursue a trade. Third, his disenchantment with the capitalist system represented by factories and the working poor created a

**CAPITALISM**—*An economic system where the means of production and distribution are privately owned and operated.*

desire to return to the land as a farmer. It is not surprising, then, that his contributions to his era fall into three areas: political, literary, and agricultural.

# The Industrial Age

Jack London lived in a time of rapid social change. The Industrial Age in America was in full swing during his adult years. Immigrants were flooding into America, creating a cheap labor pool to populate the factories. Many Americans were moving from rural areas to cities to work in factories. This mass movement created a political shift as well. The farmer was no longer the driver of the American economy. Big Business, in the form of corporations and trusts, was influencing politicians and economic policy.

These societal changes had great influence on London, who spent his earliest years living on farms and then in the city. In his youth, he labored in the factories for ten cents an hour. He shoveled coal for an unscrupulous boss who paid him the salary of one man while he unknowingly did the work of two. These experiences profoundly shaped his attitudes about society and created a strong desire to rise above his working-class status.

At one point, London became a hobo. During this time he was introduced to the ideas of Karl Marx and

**KARL MARX**—*German philosopher most noted for his analysis of history in terms of class struggle, which he expounded upon in his book* The Communist Manifesto.

socialism. Marx proposed "the abolition of private property in land; abolition of all rights of inheritance; factories, means of production, communication, and transportation to be owned by the state; and all wealth, except consumption goods, to be owned collectively."[3] When London combined his personal experience in the factories with the philosophies of Karl Marx, he grasped the essence of the socialist movement: the belief that big business taking advantage of the common worker was a hopeless system. He firmly believed that socialism was the answer to the gross abuses he saw in the factories.

London wrote frequently for the socialist cause in newsletters and magazines and gave speeches and lectures across the country.

**PROPAGANDA**— *Materials used to promote particular ideas or doctrines.*

*The Iron Heel*, a story about a socialist revolt in a futuristic society, was one of London's literary attempts to promote the cause of socialism. Unfortunately, London's tendency toward violence and gore did not match up well with the socialist's agenda of a bloodless revolution through propaganda. The socialists did not really like it.

# THE GOLDEN AGE OF MAGAZINES

London had an immense talent for writing short stories, and he had incredible luck in getting his stories into the marketplace. He was the right person with the right skills at just the right time in history. To put it in modern terms, the publishing industry was exploding and London got in on the ground floor.

The rise of industrialization gave rise to the age of magazines. The magazine industry in America reached its height at the end of the nineteenth century. From 1890 to 1915, the Golden Age of Magazines, magazine production flourished. Mass circulation, facilitated by the expanding rail system, allowed people to get news and new ideas from all over the United States. Initially, magazine content was geared toward the cultured upper classes. Newer magazines began to cater to the unrefined masses. The masses now had access to book serializations and reviews, political commentary, celebrity gossip (including London's latest exploits), and stories of national importance.

The Golden Age of Magazines gave rise to the age of advertising. Magazines were primarily financed by paid subscriptions, usually

**SERIALIZATION—** *Publishing a story in parts at regular intervals. Magazines often serialized novels by printing a new chapter in each issue.*

**11**

purchased by middle-class Americans. But the majority of the funding to pay writers came from advertising dollars. With industrialization and mass production, companies needed to find markets for all the goods coming off the production lines. Magazines were the perfect vehicles for advertising. Companies were willing to pay large sums of money to place ads in popular magazines.

**VICTORIAN AGE—** *The time of Queen Victoria's reign over the United Kingdom (1837–1901). In general, novels of that time period were stories of romance in which the woman sought the perfect domestic life with the perfect man. They often included moral lessons of right and wrong, with appropriate justice administered to each class of character.*

Although marketing data as we know it today was not available, magazine owners had a good idea of their market and catered to them. The Victorian Age, with its prim and proper romance novels, was coming to an end. There was a high demand for writers who could produce adventure stories to catch the public's interest. Part of this taste for adventure can be attributed to President Theodore Roosevelt (president from 1901–1909). An avid outdoorsman and member of the "Rough Riders" during the Spanish-American War, he exuded vitality and energy—the embodiment of rugged individualism.

Short stories in particular were in demand. They fit the magazine spacing format and could be read in one sitting.[4] Short stories tend to isolate a single person or moment and examine it, focusing on inward personal qualities. London studied the market and gave the publishers and the public what they wanted. He mastered the short story and wrote about his own adventures, giving them a realism that attracted a wide audience.

ROUGH RIDERS—*The 1st U.S. Volunteer Cavalry regiment during the Spanish-American War. Theodore Roosevelt was second in command of this regiment before becoming President.*

In addition to publishing short stories, magazines serialized novels, publishing one book chapter in each issue. Once the last chapter was published, a traditional publisher would release the novel in book form. Serialization gave the author the opportunity to attract a wider audience and to make more money— first with the magazine, then with a publisher. Using this model, London's full-length novels were serialized and his short stories were collected into books after they appeared in magazines. He worked the system to his advantage, becoming the first American author to make a million dollars from his writing.

# CONTEMPORARIES

Although London claimed that he learned his craft without the help and support of like-minded individuals, he moved in literary circles that included many

A portrait photograph of Jack London taken in 1917.

of the artists and writers popular in his day. His home, Beauty Ranch, became a local hotspot for creative types in and around San Francisco. People could drop in and stay, with complete access to his ranch. His only request was that his guests respect his work time every morning; play came in the afternoon. His hospitality was well known and appreciated by his friends and visitors.

London's local friends included George Sterling, a poet who became a close friend and confidant. He critiqued London's manuscripts and even worked on *Martin Eden*. Sterling was a good personal friend of Ambrose Bierce, best known for his short story "An Occurrence at Owl Creek Bridge." Although Sterling and Bierce were close, London could not tolerate Bierce, so the three were seldom together except on rare social occasions.

London had correspondence and personal meetings with several literary figures of the time. In 1910 and 1911, when Sinclair Lewis was just starting out, London purchased plot outlines from him. Sinclair Lewis later went on to become the first American to win the Nobel Prize for Literature.

London also corresponded with Upton Sinclair. He wrote a review of *The Jungle* as a personal favor for Sinclair. Several of London's letters to Sinclair from

1910 to 1916 can be read online at the Huntington Library website.[5]

London once wrote to Joseph Conrad after reading Conrad's *Victory*, commenting on how much he liked it. In countries like Norway and Sweden, Conrad was considered a literary type of Jack London. Conrad's novel, *The Heart of Darkness*, was set in the jungle with cannibals, akin to London's South Seas stories. Conrad did not agree with this comparison. He thought London's writing was more sensationalist than his own.[6]

## CONTRADICTIONS

Any discussion of London's work will include controversy and contradictions. London was a man of his times. The times were changing and so was he. In his early years he supported socialism. Later in life he became a practicing capitalist.

**SUFFRAGE**—*The right to vote.*

He held to the idea of white racial superiority yet often elevated the underdog in his stories. His early naturalistic plots eventually gave way to more spiritually centered stories.

**PROHIBITION**—*Law forbidding the manufacture or sale of liquor and other alcoholic beverages.*

In a lot of ways, London was ahead of his times. He supported the era's New

**16**

Woman: a woman who was empowered, independent, and free of society's traditional expectations for women. London supported women's suffrage and prohibition. He promoted

**IMPERIALISM—**
*The philosophy or practice of supporting the extension of a nation's rule over foreign countries by exercise of political or economic authority.*

American imperialism. And like President Roosevelt, he advocated land reuse and soil conservation.

## LONDON'S WORK AND CRITICAL ANALYSIS

Critics and scholars agree that London's Klondike stories are among his best works. (The Klondike is a region of Canada along the Klondike River, just east of Alaska.) His experiences there gave focus to his writing. His vivid depictions of life in the Northland draw readers into the story. These are the stories that brought him worldwide fame.

London eventually grew tired of writing about the Klondike, but his readers clamored for more. He obliged at first, but quickly expanded into other areas such as reporting and nonfiction books. London's Hawaiian stories were received well enough, as were his short stories from the South Seas. But London ran into trouble when he wrote novels, partly because his work was rarely simple entertainment.

**17**

He often wrote to espouse an ideology or his current philosophy, or to carry out a personal agenda. He admitted, "I will sacrifice form *every time*, when it boils down to a final question of choice between form and matter. The thought is the thing."[7] He willingly sacrificed the form of novel writing to get his philosophical points across.

Because of London's tendency to preach his life's philosophy through his stories, many of his later books received only lukewarm receptions from contemporary critics. However, modern scholarship looks at the late stories differently, taking into account the philosophical and cultural content only evident from the perspective of history. Modern scholars also have access to a huge store of London's personal papers, correspondence, and annotated books from his personal library. Comparing his writing to his personal notes reveals a lot of what drove London in his writing at any given time. These more intimate looks into the man were not available to his contemporary critics.

## COMMON THEMES

Much of London's early work falls into the category of Naturalism. Naturalism as a literary genre was shaped by the emerging discoveries and theories of science. Naturalism assumes a person's life is determined strictly by his surroundings and genetics. The individual does not have a spirit but lives completely within the physical realm of nature. This style is particularly evident in London's Klondike stories, where nature is depicted as an antagonist and much of the action includes the interaction between man and nature.

As an extension of Naturalism, London liked to intertwine intellect and instinct. He masters this interplay in *The Call of the Wild*, where the dog Buck comes into the wilderness with intellect but has to develop his instincts. London identifies the intellect with civilization and instinct with the wilderness. This interplay is also evident in *White Fang*. The dog White Fang functions mainly on instinct in the wilderness but develops intellectually as he is drawn farther and farther into the civilized world.

London also promoted his views on Social Darwinism. Social Darwinism is the idea that Darwin's theory of evolution can be applied to whole societies.[8] London believed that just as animals evolve, societies evolve. He plays out this theme in many of his Klondike stories. For example, to survive in the Northland, one "must be prepared to forget many of the things he has learned, and to acquire such customs as are inherent with existence in the new land;

**DARWINISM**—*Theory of evolution through natural selection popularized by Charles Darwin in his book* Origin of the Species.

. . . and oftentimes he must reverse the very codes by which his conduct has hitherto been shaped."[9] In London's Northland, if a person does not adapt to his new society, he fails. This failure inevitably leads to death, leaving only those best able to adapt to carry on in society.

Social Darwinism, taken to its logical conclusion, leads to the idea that through natural selection there is a hierarchy of societies. Social Darwinists usually identified societies by race. London promoted the idea of Anglo-Saxon superiority to justify American imperialism.[10] Even though he held to these beliefs, he often found that which was admirable in these so-called inferior races. His portrayal of Indians in the Klondike show his sensitivity to their plight of losing their homeland to the settlers. Still later, in his Hawaiian fiction, London demonstrates empathy for the islanders who lost their lands to the invading British.

**ANGLO-SAXON SUPERIORITY—**
*A Social Darwinist theory that the early settlers of the United States (especially those from Britain and Germany) were of a superior race of people. Being superior, they were destined to dominate other peoples and cultures.*

Although death is not a theme per se in London's works, he never shied away from depicting it in his writings, often making a character's death central to the progression of the story. Because of the vivid depictions of violence and gore, so foreign to the Victorian mind, he earned the title "Father of Red-Blooded American Literature."[11] *The Call of the Wild* is filled with red imagery, from the bloodless red sweater of Buck's first tamer to the red blood in Buck's mouth as he kills his prey in the final chapter. White Fang, too, becomes a master at drawing blood from his enemies. A typical example of London's prose is the description of the seal slaughter in *The Sea-Wolf:* "After a good day's killing I have seen our decks covered with hides and bodies, slippery with fat and blood, the scuppers running red; masts, ropes, and rails spattered with the sanguinary color; and the men, like butchers plying their trade, naked and red of arm and hand, hard at work with ripping and flensing knives, removing the skins from the pretty sea creatures they had killed."[12] Although the character in the book is appalled by the gore, it is the writer who seems to like it.

## CHARACTER TYPES

The significant themes in London's writing can be analyzed by tracing the social, physical, and psychological changes in his main characters. An overall analysis of his work shows that his main concerns tended to be class issues, reflecting his own rise from working class to the middle class; physical beauty,

**21**

strength, and intellect as signs of superiority; and nature as antagonist or healing retreat.

London's heroes are often supermen, using brawn or intellect to accomplish their purpose. The main character either possesses these traits when introduced, or the plot is about how the main character acquires them. For example, Humphrey Van Weyden in *The Sea-Wolf* acquires brawn and Martin Eden, in the novel of the same name, refines his intellect. This interplay between brawn and intellect probably comes from London's own experiences as he moved from working in the factories to becoming more of an intellectual.

Another element in London's writings is the feminist heroine, embodied in the era's New Woman. London's heroines, such as Frona Welse in *A Daughter of the Snows*, demonstrated great physical prowess.[13] This was shocking to the Victorian mind accustomed to the pure, protected, virginal heroines of the late nineteenth-century novels.

London's second wife, Charmian Kitteredge, was the embodiment of the New Woman. She and London shared equally in their relationship, an uncommon arrangement in that day and age. Each of London's Anglo-Saxon heroines created after he met her is a reflection of Charmian in some way.

London had the unique ability to write about

nature in such a way as to give it a life and character of its own. He animated the dead of winter as the White Silence in his Klondike stories and made nature the main character in his story "All Gold Canyon." This type of characterization fit in well with his penchant for naturalism.

# SETTING

London also used nature powerfully in setting. Through vivid description, he could intensify the narrative, provide a sensory experience, or foreshadow events in a story. A lot of his stories depend heavily upon a specific geographic location for effect, whether on the open sea, on a hot tropical island, in the frozen Northland, or in a peaceful California valley. And because most of his stories take place about the time he was alive, his settings provide breadth and depth to modern historical interpretations of his work.

# COMMON LITERARY DEVICES

Irony and hyperbole both played roles in London's writing. He often used irony to show the insensitivity of American imperialists as they took over land and peoples. Sometimes his irony would hit a nerve and he would suffer for revealing some of the activities taking place during the process. However, he never apologized for his stories, claiming the right of a fiction writer to tell a good story.

London's most famous work, *The Call of the Wild*, uses anthropomorphism, giving human characteristics to animals. By using animals, he allows the reader to regress along with Buck from civilization to the wild. The reader can easily apply the process to humans, but the sheer brutality of the humans to the dogs and the dogs to each other is easier to accept when observed in the animal world.

Contrast became a favorite tool for London. He liked to show processes in reverse, or the flip side of character under pressure. Instead of using contrast within stories, he would conceive two entirely different stories. *The Call of the Wild*, the story of a tame dog from California regressing to the wild, is in complete contrast to *White Fang*, the story of a wild dog from the Yukon being tamed. Within his first book of short stories, *The Son of the Wolf*, the half-breed Malemute Kid is contrasted with lesser men like Carter Weatherbee and Percy Cuthfert. The Kid lives by a code of ethics based on survival and camaraderie. Weatherbee and Cuthfert end up killing each other during the White Silence of a Yukon winter because of selfishness.

# NARRATIVE STYLE

Jack London's personal experiences brought to his writing a realism that was lacking in the short stories typical of the late 1800s. He directed his stories to his audience: the working class. His plain talk and direct, sometimes violent depictions of events contrasted sharply with the Victorian romance novel.

Several factors played into the making of Jack London both as a man and a writer: poverty, his many adventures, manual labor in various factories, time in jail, and a trip to the Yukon. He had the gift of turning the meat of his experiences through fiction, making them come alive for many who would never experience these things themselves. His audience loved it.

# THE MAKING OF A WRITER

Jack London was born John Griffith Chaney on January 12, 1876, in San Francisco, California. Jack's mother, Flora Wellman, claimed William H. Chaney as his father. Flora and Chaney had been living together at the time of conception, but Chaney denied he was the father and deserted Flora soon after she announced she was pregnant.

After the birth, Flora was too weak to nurse Jack. She hired a wet nurse (a woman to breastfeed Jack in her place), Virginia "Jennie" Prentiss. Jennie became a surrogate mother for Jack, providing the love and comfort his mother would not. Jack visited Jennie often during his youth and they became life-long friends.

# EARLY YEARS IN THE COUNTRY

Eight months after Jack was born, Flora married a Civil War veteran, John London. Until this time, Jack had been living with the Prentisses. When Flora remarried, Jack came to live with his mother, John, and John's two young daughters, Eliza and Ida. Eliza, only eight at the time, did most of the mothering for Jack during his childhood. Jack turned to her throughout his life for advice and other help.

Jack's father, John, tried his hand at farming and was somewhat successful with a small plot of land in Oakland. At Flora's urging, they moved to a larger farm in the country. After several starts at various farms, each bigger than the last, they ran into hard times and lost everything. Like many others during the Industrial Age, they moved to the city to find work.

# OAKLAND AND THE BAY AREA

When Jack was about nine years old, the family returned to Oakland. They lived in poverty, frequently moving from house to house as necessity dictated. Jack's childhood days consisted of school,

A portrait photograph of a nine-year-old Jack London, taken in 1885.

work, and fighting. While Jack attended school, he worked various jobs to supplement the family income. He worked as a newsboy, loaded ice wagons, swept saloons, and set up pins in a bowling alley. He also learned to fight. He was known as a solid fighter and needed only the slightest provocation to spark a brawl.

In Oakland, Jack discovered a treasure—the Oakland Free Library. The librarian, Ina Coolbrith, took a personal interest in Jack's intellectual development and helped guide him to suitable books to read. She describes Jack as "coming into the library with a bundle of newspapers under his arm, badly poised, looking poor, shabby, and uncared for, asking for something good to read, and wanting to consume every book that had an interesting title."[1] Some of his first books were Washington Irving's *Tales of the Alhambra* and Horatio Alger's stories. These adventure and rags-to-riches stories fanned the flames of Jack's desire to move up the social ladder and out of his narrow world.

London read voraciously while walking to and from school, while eating, and any time of day he could. Later in life, he observed that there were probably very few books in that library that were not, at one time or another, checked out under the name Jack London. He told his sister he wanted to one day have

Jack London at age nine with his dog, Rollo.

a house with one whole room devoted to books. He eventually ended up with several rooms of books.

Another of Jack's loves was the water. He began sailing with his stepfather around San Francisco Bay at a young age. By twelve years old, he could competently maneuver his skiff (a small rowboat with a sail) around the bay. He finished eighth grade at Cole Grammar School, but since the family needed money, he went to work in a cannery (a canning factory), putting an end to his formal schooling. The hours at the factory were long and grueling. Although only fourteen years old by this time, London developed a strong dislike for the mind-numbing life of a "work beast." To escape the drudgery, he turned to the taverns along the waterfront. Here he picked up the habit of drinking and heard fascinating stories from the men who worked the seas. He began to make a distinction in his mind between those he considered to be real men who really "lived" and those who stayed in the cities, bound to mindless work in the factories or growing soft in the genteel classes. These class distinctions would come to play an important part in many of his works.

Jack soon left the cannery to pursue adventure out on the bay. He borrowed three hundred dollars from Jenny Prentiss and bought a boat called the *Razzle Dazzle*. He became a juvenile delinquent, raiding private oyster beds. In those days, the railroad companies held monopolies on many businesses. They owned the rights to harvest oysters in the San Francisco Bay. Deciding this was unfair, some men took to raiding the oyster beds and selling the oysters to the waterfront bars and markets for large profits. The railroad monopolies were not well liked, so public opinion favored the oyster pirates.

After about three months, the mainsail of his sloop burned in an accidental fire. London opted to join the California Fish Patrol, enforcing the law against the very people he used to work with. He found that his new associates drank even more than his pirating buddies, and he joined right in. In his sober moments, he began to see the need for a change of direction in his life.

## OUT TO SEA

In 1893, London signed on to the *Sophie Sutherland* as an able-bodied seaman for an eight-month sealing voyage. The trip took him to Hawaii, the Bonin Islands, Japan, and the Bering Sea. London finally had his chance to see the world that he had only read about. The ports, indeed, were exotic, but the up-close view of killing seals for profit balanced out Jack's romantic views of sea faring. His attitude toward sealing shows through the comments of Humphrey

Van Weyden in *The Sea-Wolf*. "It was wanton slaughter, and all for woman's sake."[2] The seal fur was used to make women's clothing.

On the sea London learned the value of daily discipline and routine, which he incorporated into his professional life as a writer. When he finally began to write for a living, he committed to write one thousand words a day, regardless of his health or where he was at the time. By keeping this commitment he was able to produce fifty books and hundreds of short stories, essays, and articles in just sixteen years.

## THE WORK BEAST

Upon return from the sea voyage, London came to realize that most of his former friends were either dead, in jail, or hiding from the law. And he wanted to live. London determined to change his life but faced the reality of a nationwide depression. Factories closed, banks folded, and thousands were without jobs. He returned to being a work beast, working in a jute mill making ropes for ten cents an hour.

During this time, his mother noticed a contest in the *San Francisco Morning Call* newspaper for youth writers. She encouraged London to enter. He did, writing a story titled "Story of a Typhoon Off the Coast of Japan," based on his experiences aboard the *Sophie Sutherland*. With only an eighth-grade education he won first prize: twenty-five dollars and publication in the newspaper. The second and third place winners were college students from the University of California and Stanford University. This was London's first experience with turning his life experiences into cash. Many of his youthful adventures would resurface in his writing, turning his life into story.

During the Industrial Age, the general belief was that anyone could move up in a company through hard, honest work, rising through the ranks to one day become a partner in the firm. Believing this and having the good fortune to find a foreman with the same views, London took a job shoveling coal in a power plant. His boss indicated that within a couple of years London could achieve his dream. After a few weeks of intense manual labor, London found out his boss had deceived him. He was doing the work of two men and being paid the wages of one. He quit immediately, angry and disillusioned. He now became one of the tens of thousands of unemployed workers in the United States. At eighteen, he was lower on the socio-economic scale than when he had started working.

# RIDING THE RAILS TO SOCIALISM

London decided to join Jacob Coxey's Industrial Army, a nationwide rally of unemployed men who planned to march on the capital in Washington, DC. London caught up with the California contingent in the Sierra Nevada Mountains, traveling as a hobo on the rails as he had learned two years earlier from a group of homeless youth. While moving East with these men, London heard many discussions about socialism versus capitalism. He sided with the socialist point of view, agreeing with the idea that capitalism ignored the human needs of the masses in the interests of a greedy few at the top. He had already experienced the bottom of the Social Pit, as he called it, and could identify with those near the bottom of the social hierarchy.

Like many others facing this long march without much food or shelter, he deserted Coxey's Army. London went to Chicago, visiting some of his mother's relatives before moving on to New York and Niagara Falls. After a single visit to the falls and one night in a field, he was arrested for vagrancy, or homelessness. The judge, accustomed to many of these types of arrests, showed no mercy and sentenced him to thirty days on a chain gang at the Erie County Penitentiary.

Here, London saw first-hand the awful conditions of the United States' prisons of that time. There were no human rights considered. The castoffs of society ended up here, enduring brutality and degradation in a world governed by might. People got what they wanted through sheer physical force. It was here that London became convinced that salvation for the masses would come from socialism, and for the individual through intellectual power. He resolved "to sell no more muscle, and to become a vendor of brains."[3] He decided that education was the best way to achieve this goal.

## BACK TO SCHOOL

When London returned to Oakland in 1895, he enrolled in high school at the age of nineteen. He stayed for about a year before dropping out. During his time in high school he joined the Henry Clay [debating] Club, befriended Herman "Jim" Whitaker, who taught him boxing and fencing, and was frequently published in the school magazine *The High School Aegis*. He also returned to the Oakland Free Library, where he came across a copy of Karl Marx's *Communist Manifesto*. He quickly identified with Marx's philosophy of rule by the working class rather than rule by the factory owners and big businessmen. His experiences at work and with poverty fostered a zeal for social reform, a theme that appears frequently in his writing. In 1896 he joined the Socialist Labor Party and became known as the "Boy Socialist" of Oakland. London was known for his fiery speeches in the public squares. He ran for mayor of Oakland on the Socialist Labor Party ticket twice, although he did not win.

His interest in politics and his foray into his own intellectual development opened a new world to him—middle-class society. He was invited into the homes of those who sympathized with the socialist cause. One family in particular took him in, the Applegarths. Their daughter, Mabel, became the model for the love interest in *Martin Eden*.

After his high school experience, London decided to attend college. Since he had not completed high school, he entered into a program of self-study. He passed the entrance exams for the University of California at Berkeley. It was here that he read Herbert Spencer's books that tied Darwin's theory of evolution to social processes. Spencer's idea came to be known as Social Darwinism, the idea that societies evolve with the result that some are superior to others.

London soon realized that at twenty years old, he had more life experience than most of his professors and he was learning more on his own. London came to the conclusion that it was not worth trying to attend school and support his family members. After one semester, London dropped out of the university.

When he left Berkeley, he wanted to try to make a living as a writer. He had had many discussions on becoming a writer with his friends in the debating club. He rented a typewriter and threw himself wholeheartedly into the endeavor. For months, the rejection slips piled up. No one was buying what he had to sell. Out of money, he went to work in the laundry of a military school, once again entering the ranks of the work beast. He was saved from this drudgery by a surprise twist of fate.

## ADVENTURE IN THE KLONDIKE

Gold! The Klondike Gold Rush was on. During the summer of 1896, a group of miners discovered rich gold deposits in the rivers of Canada's Yukon Territory. Miners already in the area rushed to stake claims along the rivers. When some of these miners arrived in San Francisco on July 15 and in Seattle on July 17, 1897, it set off a stampede for America's last great gold rush. Jack London heard the call and turned to his sister for backing.

Eliza's husband, Captain James H. Shepard, agreed to go north with London to seek their fortunes. Eliza and Captain Shepard funded the venture

A reconstruction of Jack London's Canadian cabin
during his days as a prospector as it stands today in
London Square, Oakland.

by mortgaging their home and using their savings. London and Shepard started their journey in the summer of 1897.

Only two months into the deal, Shepard decided he was not up to this adventure physically and left London with supplies and money to finish the trip without him. London staked a claim near Dawson, where he stayed during the long Arctic winter. It was during this long winter that he came to grips with his life. He wrote, "It was in the Klondike that I found myself. There, nobody talks. Everybody thinks. You get your perspective. I got mine."[4] He made up his mind to pursue his dreams instead of returning to a life of manual labor. He left the Yukon Territory as soon as the spring thaw occurred, suffering from scurvy, a disease caused by a lack of vitamin C. He already had the early symptoms of swollen, bleeding gums and loose teeth. This would be the first of many instances where health problems cut his adventures short.

Most of London's stories have some personal-experience elements to them. London romanticized many of his physical hardships and challenges in his stories. For example, he described his actual experience going through the White Horse Rapids in his article "Through the Rapids on the Way to Klondike."

The romanticized version appears in his book *Smoke Bellew*.[5]

This intense, one-year period accounts for London's second life change. London's transformation occurred during the long, sunless winter he describes in his stories as the White Silence. During this phase London did not find gold, but he acquired a gold mine of material for his future as a writer. He told stories and listened to the stories of others, both travelers and locals, stoking the fire of his imagination. The Klondike proved a rich source for the early success that would bring him worldwide fame.

# THE NORTHLAND STORIES

L ondon's determination to better his station in life was put to the test immediately. Upon returning home in June 1898, he found out his stepfather had died. He was now responsible for supporting his entire household. Still not certain of his prospects as a writer, London applied for a job at the post office. He took the civil service exam and, while waiting to hear the results, he resolved to try writing again.

## A TRICKLE OF INTEREST

In 1898 London published more than twenty pieces of writing, mostly articles. He sent manuscripts to *The Youth's Companion*, *Black Cat* magazine, and *The Overland Monthly*. *The Youth's Companion* turned him down, but *The Overland Monthly,* a Western literary magazine, accepted "To the Man on Trail" for ten dollars.

Shortly after that, *Black Cat* accepted his four-thousand-word story "A Thousand Deaths" for forty dollars, provided he would give them permission to cut it in half. London was thrilled. "I told Mr. Umbstaetter he could cut it down two-halves if he'd only send the money along. He did, by return mail."[1]

When "To the Man on Trail" came out in January 1899, London was offered a job at the post office paying forty dollars a month. This was a small fortune compared to his ten cents an hour working in the jute mill. However, based on his two meager successes with writing, he turned the job down. It turned out to be a wise decision. *The Overland Monthly* sale proved to be London's big break. Houghton Mifflin, one of America's most prestigious publishers at that time, took note of his work and offered to publish a collection of his short stories about the Northland. The book, *The Son of the Wolf* (1900), was one of Houghton Mifflin's best selling books of 1900.[2] On the day it was published, London married Bessie Maddern, his first wife.

Most of *The Son of the Wolf* stories center on a young half-breed known as the Malemute Kid. The Kid lives by the Northland code, and old-timers and newcomers alike look up to him. The code—a lifestyle of compassion, camaraderie, integrity, self-lessness, and situational justice—derives from living through what London terms the White Silence. Some of his most memorable descriptions depict this time of winter:

> Nature has many tricks wherewith she convinces man of his finity—the ceaseless flow of the tides, the fury of the storm, the shock of the earthquake, the long roll of heaven's artillery—but the most tremendous, the most stupefying of all, is the passive phase of the White Silence. All movement ceases, the sky clears, the heavens are as brass; the slightest whisper seems sacrilege, and man becomes timid, affrighted at the sound of his own voice. Sole speck of life journeying across the ghostly wastes of a dead world, he trembles at his audacity, realizes that his is a maggot's life, nothing more.[3]

Throughout the White Silence, men must rely on each other to survive. They live in small spaces, sharing whatever stock of food and entertainment each has to offer. As with any frontier without a regular police force, the Northland uses frontier justice to keep the peace. London consistently uses this Northland code as a measuring stick of character.

Malemute Kid, who is the "high priest of the code,"[4] keeps his head during every crisis and effortlessly applies the code to whatever situation he is in. In "To the Man on Trail," he allows a man who has stolen forty thousand dollars from a gambling house to escape by helping him, yet does nothing to aide the Canadian Mounted Police officer who is tracking the thief. His buddies are astounded. Then they learn from the Kid that the man's partner had run off with the money and gambled it away. He was simply getting his money back. He took no more than what he was owed.

Again in "The Men of Forty-Mile," the Kid administers justice to two men ready to fight a duel because of a petty argument about whether the river ice is formed on top of the water or at the bottom of the river. The Kid sets it up so that whoever wins the duel gets hanged for murder. Both men sheepishly withdraw from the duel and justice is served.

In contrast to the Malemute Kid, the two men in "In a Far Country," Carter Weatherbee and Percy Cuthfert, end up killing each other during the White Silence. At first, they perform their tasks of survival with a spirit of camaraderie. That quickly fades as they become petty and suspicious. They end up killing each other over their sugar supply. When measured against the Northland Code, they fail miserably. London labels them "Incapables" and holds them up as examples of those who cannot or will not adapt.

# A FLOOD OF SUCCESS

Success came rapidly after publication of *The Son of the Wolf*. London had found his voice, tapping into the

Klondike scenery today is just as breathtaking in its natural beauty as it was in the time of Jack London.

thoughts and feelings of the working class. He studied his markets and knew them well. He proceeded to exploit the market for material gain. He did not hoard his money but used it for his grandiose plans and various adventures that needed funding. Writing became his means to an end. He was known as a generous man and he supported three separate households: his, his mother's, and eventually that of Bessie and his two daughters.

Writing for money highlighted some of the paradoxes in London's socialist philosophies. Even though he was a socialist, he wrote rags-to-riches stories along the lines of Horatio Alger. London himself moved from the working class to the middle class. This rise became problematic for London as a socialist. Later in life, although he still claimed to be a socialist , he lived the life of a rich capitalist. He owned a large ranch complete with hired hands and servants.

After *The Son of the Wolf,* two other short story collections, *The God of His Fathers* (1901) and *Children of the Frost* (1902), were published by Century. *The God of His Fathers* runs in a vein similar to *The Son of the Wolf* except the central character is Sitka Charley, another half-breed with exceptional character.

With *Children of the Frost*, London decided to play with contrasts. He presents a series of Northland stories from the natives' point of view. London is careful to avoid the stereotypes of Indians so often found in stories of the Wild West. Instead, he presents them as loyal, honest, and self-sacrificing. The Indians are often more noble and admirable than the vicious Anglo-Saxon characters in these stories.

All three of these Northland books promote London's ideas on Social Darwinism and Anglo-Saxon superiority. Because this idea was prevalent at the time, both editors and readers tended to overlook this non-inappropriate strain of thinking. His sympathetic treatment of the natives may have helped, too.

## "TO BUILD A FIRE"

Another Klondike story, "To Build a Fire," has become one of America's most reprinted short stories. London actually had two versions of this story published. The 1902 version was published in May in *The Youth's Companion*. In this version, the resourceful main character survives a fall into icy water. In the better-known 1910 version, the protagonist lacks the survival skills he needs and perishes because of his own foolishness. It is this later version that is found in many literature books.

**PROTAGONIST—** *The main character in a novel or other piece of writing.*

# PLOT SUMMARY, 1910 VERSION

The story opens as a man with only a dog for a companion sets out for a ten-mile trek to a neighboring claim in the Klondike. It is seventy degrees below zero, which means it is one hundred degrees below freezing. But the man does not know this. The unnamed man tests the temperature by spitting in the air. He knows that spit will crackle on the snow at fifty below, but his spit solidifies while still in the air. He is surprised, and realizes it must be colder than fifty below, but continues on anyway.

The man, a newcomer, has been warned by an old-timer not to go out alone when the temperature drops past fifty degrees below zero. By ignoring this warning, he sets the stage for his inevitable demise. As London writes in the story, "The trouble with him was that he was without imagination. He was quick and alert in the things of life, but only in the things, and not in the significances."[5] He was practical, but did not look for the deeper meanings in life.

Man and beast continue on the trail, with the fact of the cold registering on the man's mind periodically. He is intent on scanning his surroundings for hidden springs of water beneath the ice and the snow, the biggest threat to travelers. He comes across several of these but is able to avoid them. The dog is depressed by the cold, constantly expecting the man to seek shelter or build a fire.

Stopping for lunch at half past noon, the man takes his glove off to retrieve his lunch, which is stored inside his shirt next to his skin to keep it from freezing. Immediately, his exposed fingers become numb. Once again, he registers surprise. The numbness and the ice around his mouth on his beard keep him from being able to eat. He chuckles at himself for forgetting to build a fire to melt the ice from his face and keep his hands warm while he holds his food. He mentally acknowledges that the old-timer from Sulphur Creek spoke the truth about the winters in the Klondike.

The man resumes his trip and then it happens. He breaks through some ice without warning, getting wet from his feet half way to his knees. To survive, he must stop and build a fire. He knows he must not fail, as the old-timer has warned him. His fire built, he smiles at the old-timer laying down the law about no one going out alone after fifty below zero. The narrator notes, "Well, here he was; he had had the accident; he was alone; and he had saved himself."[6] But he had made a mistake. He built the fire under a spruce tree. As the fire gets going, snow falls from the branches and puts the fire out. He immediately realizes the significance. He "was shocked. It was as though he had just heard his own sentence of death."[7] He must build another fire.

Through much difficulty and using all his matches, he manages to get a second fire going. But his numb body will not cooperate and his shivering hands scatter the burning wood. Both the fire and his hope are extinguished. He briefly considers killing his dog and using the carcass for warmth, but the dog's instincts tell him something is wrong and he avoids the man.

Fear of death overtakes the man and he begins to run along the trail. He collapses several times, finally realizing that he cannot continue. In his practical way, he acknowledges that he will die. As he sits in the snow to die with dignity, he mumbles to the old-timer on Sulphur Creek, "You were right, old hoss; you were right."[8]

# LITERARY DEVICES

London's plotting of this story is very tight. Every sentence in the story moves it toward its conclusion, and every element speaks to the outcome. The story focuses on just one day, and the beginning, middle, and end are clearly identifiable. A man leaves on a journey, filled with arrogance. He suffers a fatal fall through the ice. He admits his mistake before dying with dignity.

The interplay of literary devices is what makes this story so compelling. London sets the atmosphere from the first paragraph using phrases like "exceedingly cold and gray," "dim and little-traveled trail," "intangible pall," and "subtle gloom." The reader can immediately guess that the man is doomed. This imagery, often associated with the White Silence in his other stories, is repeated throughout the story to keep the underlying dread constant.

The technique of flashback shows the main character's progressive realization that he is doomed. The man enters into an ongoing mental dialogue with the old-timer on Sulphur Creek. He recalls the old-timer's advice—initially laughing at it, then realizing its truth.

London's choices in sequencing the events are excellent. He could have started the story with the actual conversation, allowing the reader to meet the wise old man. Instead, London uses the man's internal dialogue with the old timer to show his slow but sure acceptance of the truth: No one should travel alone once the temperature drops to fifty degrees below zero.

# THEME

London picks up one of his favorite Klondike themes in this story: the failure of those who lack imagination to survive in a cold and indifferent world. Although the dog is not a main character, London contrasts the dog's instinct with the man's intelligence. London makes the point that instinct is more important for survival than intellect.

Because the man lacks imagination, his concrete observations of his situation are not enough to save him. This is evidenced in his surprise when his spit crackles in the air instead of on the ground, and then again when the cold freezes his hands as he tries to eat without first building a fire. His mere observations have not alerted him to the seriousness of his situation. What was merely surprise before turns into shock when snow falls on his fire, then to terror when his second fire dies, signaling his imminent demise. Once the facts are clear, the man turns back upon his practical side. He simply sits down to die, admitting his failure.

# OTHER WRITING/PERSONAL LIFE

Two other books were published during 1902. One was yet another Northland story, *A Daughter of the*

*Snows*. This was London's first novel and it was not very good. Even London did not like it, realizing "I squandered into it enough stuff for a dozen novels."[9] McClure's, the publisher who promised to publish anything London wrote for them, did not think it was very good, either. McClure's kept its word by passing it off to the publisher J.P. Lippincott. The other book published in 1902 was a collection of juvenile stories based on London's adventures on San Francisco Bay titled *Tales of the Fish Patrol*.

During the flurry of publishing activity in 1902, London's marriage began to show signs of stress. Even so, London wrote his most famous novel, *The Call of the Wild*, during this time. Although his marriage was failing, his career was about to take off.

# CHAPTER 4

# A Dog Story

By this time in his career, London had a working relationship with George Brett of Macmillan Publishing. Macmillan had already published three of London's books, none of which sold very well. Instead of the usual royalties contract, Brett offered to buy *The Call of the Wild* for a one-time payment of two thousand dollars. In exchange, he would be able to print the book immediately and then promote the book with special bindings, illustrations, and advertising. Otherwise, it would be a couple of years before the book would be printed, with royalties coming even later than that.

London's earlier books combined had not even earned him a thousand dollars. Weighing the option of a badly needed two thousand dollars now or waiting a couple of years for an undetermined amount of money, London chose the flat fee for the book.

*The Call of the Wild* was a surprise hit, even to Macmillan. Serialized in the *Saturday Evening Post*, it sold out its first ten thousand copies in the first day.[1] Critics compared London to Rudyard Kipling, Bret Harte, and Stephen Crane. The book had hit a nerve with the American people and would soon touch the imaginations of an international audience.

Although the book would have eventually made over one hundred thousand dollars in royalties for London, he never regretted his decision to accept only two thousand dollars. London understood the value of what had occurred. He knew there was no price tag for what he eventually gained from Brett's marketing arrangement. From this point forward, London was able to demand top dollar for all of his writing.

## STRUCTURE

*The Call of the Wild* is divided into seven chapters. Detailing the life of a dog, Buck, these chapters can be divided into sections related to the stages of the mythical hero: a call to adventure, departure, initiation, transformation, and return. Buck's development clearly follows these stages as he goes from being household pet of a California judge to legendary ghost dog in the frozen Northland.

# PLOT SUMMARY

## Chapter 1—Into the Primitive

The story takes place in the early days of the Yukon Gold Rush of 1898. Buck, a St. Bernard and Scotch shepherd mix, leads a comfortable life on the estate of Judge Miller in California. One of the judge's servants steals Buck and sells him to a dog trader. Buck is sent to the Yukon Territory for use as a sled dog.

Abused on his train trip, Buck turns into a red-eyed,

**Marshall and Louis Bond are photographed with their dog, Jack, outside of their Dawson City cabin. The dog would serve as a model for Buck in *The Call of the Wild*.**

**57**

vicious animal by the time he arrives in Seattle. His next master, for a short while, is a man in a red sweater with a club. This man repeatedly fends off Buck's attacks through use of the club. Thus, Buck learns the first lesson of primitive existence: The law of the club, that "a man with a club is a lawgiver, a master to be obeyed, but not necessarily conciliated."[2]

Thoroughly subdued, Buck is sold to a Frenchman, Perrault, and is taken aboard ship to head even further North. Perrault works carrying dispatches for the Canadian government. On board ship, Buck meets other dogs that will be on Perrault's dogsled team: Curly, Dave, and Spitzbergen (Spitz for short). At their first meal, Spitz steals a bone from Buck's meal, creating an immediate tension between the two dogs. The ship docks and the dogs are brought out into the cold.

## Chapter 2—The Law of Club and Fang

Buck's first impressions of the port town of Dyea involve fear, savagery, and confusion. Buck's second lesson comes when a husky attacks Curly as she tries to be friendly. When Curly hits the ground, a group of huskies converge on her, tearing her to pieces. Buck learns another important lesson of the wild: "No fair play. Once down, that was the end of you."[3]

An illustration of Buck that ran in the 1903 edition of
*The Call of the Wild.*

Buck almost immediately begins his life of toil in the traces, the straps and harnesses used to control the sled dog team. He quickly learns how to work as part of a team and how to survive in the wilderness. He learns what it is to be hungry. His food ration never seems to be enough and when he does not eat fast enough, the other dogs steal his food. He watches the other dogs and learns to steal food, not only from the other dogs but from Perrault's cooking stash as well. This descent marks his move from "the law of love and fellowship" that Buck knew in the Southland to his adaptation to "the law of club and fang" in the primitive North. Buck will be a survivor because he adapts.

## Chapter 3—The Dominant Primordial Beast

This chapter describes the inevitable battle when Spitz and Buck fight for leadership. When they finally face off Buck begins fighting by instinct. Spitz, wiser in the ways of the wild, lets Buck wear himself out with rush after rush. When Buck stumbles, with a pack of sixty dogs surrounding him, he realizes he must keep on his feet, so he changes his tactics. He begins to fight with his intellect. He rushes Spitz and breaks one of Spitz's forelegs. Again, he rushes and breaks the other. One last hit and Spitz is on the ground. With the pack moving in, "Buck stood and looked on, the successful champion, the dominant primordial beast who had made his kill and found it good."[4]

**PRIMORDIAL—**
*Being primary, or happening first, in time.*

## Chapter 4—Who Has Won to Mastership

The next morning, Francois and Perrault cannot find Spitz but deduce from Buck's wounds what has happened. Buck takes leadership of the team and proves himself worthy. When they return to Skaguay, the two men are sent on another assignment and the team is turned over to other drivers who work the mail run. These new drivers are fair, but the dogs grow weary. At night, Buck lies by the fire and dreams of the warm Southland and all that he knew there, as in a distant memory. He also dreams of a squat, hairy man tending a fire, an even more distant memory of ancestors long gone. Buck's dreams throughout the story signal how far he is along the path to the primitive.

## Chapter 5—The Toil of Trace and Trail

Upon their return to Skaguay, the dogs are too exhausted to be of much use for the mail runs. They are sold to three Americans, Hal, Charles and

A photograph of a modern dogsled team at work.
Dogsleds are normally pulled by 10-12 dogs.

Mercedes. Upon seeing the condition of their camp, "tent half-stretched, dishes unwashed, everything in disorder,"[5] Buck knew these people were out of place in the Northland. When it is time to take off, the dogs are unable to move their overloaded and top-heavy sled. Hal decides the dogs are lazy and proceeds to whip them mercilessly.

The trio's incompetence continues throughout the journey. Eventually, the group pulls in to John Thornton's camp at the mouth of the White River. Thornton warns them that the river ice is too thin and should be avoided. Hal and crew decide to continue on. The usual beating is required to get the team going, but Buck refuses to get up. His instincts warn him of some impending doom so he lies still. Thornton, who has witnessed the beating, puts a stop to it and angrily frees Buck from the traces. Buck and Thornton watch as the party goes out onto the river, only to break through the ice and disappear beneath the water.

## Chapter 6—For the Love of a Man

John Thornton becomes Buck's new master, treating him with love and kindness. As Buck recuperates under his care, Buck comes to love Thornton and becomes his protector and defender. But London points out that "the strain of the primitive, which the Northland had aroused in him, remained alive and active."

Buck continues to dream and starts to identify with "shades of all manner of dogs, half-wolves and wild wolves"[6] that lurk about him in the night. London explains, "Deep in the forest a call was sounding . . ."[7] Buck runs toward the forest to answer the call, but each time love for Thornton brings him back.

## Chapter 7—The Sounding of the Call

Eventually, Thornton leaves the settlements and goes deep into the wilderness in search of a fabled, lost gold mine. After a year of wandering, Thornton and his companions find gold and begin to mine it, earning thousands of dollars a day. Buck still dreams of the short-legged hairy man, and he still hears the call in the forest. Buck starts returning to the forest more and more often for longer and longer periods. He becomes "a killer, a thing that preyed, living on the things that lived, unaided, alone, by virtue of his own strength and prowess, surviving triumphantly in a hostile environment where only the strong survive."[8]

One day Buck returns to camp and finds it has been attacked by the local Yeehat Indians. All the men and dogs have been killed. The Yeehats are in the midst of celebrating their success when Buck attacks them.  Because of his love for Thornton, Buck rages through the group, killing as many as he can. The rest flee ". . . proclaiming as they fled the advent of the Evil Spirit."[9] With Thornton gone, "The last tie was broken. Man and the claims of man no longer bound him."[10] Buck answers the call. He returns to the forest and locates the pack of the wolf he befriended the previous year. Buck is accepted into the pack and runs with them from then on.

**64**

An illustration of Buck leaping into the air, created by artist Paul Bransom for the 1903 edition of *The Call of the Wild*.

Over time, the Yeehats notice that the wolf pack begins to take on some new characteristics. These traits are similar to those of the fierce evil one they had seen in the valley of the miners. This dog gets the blame for many of their misfortunes, including dead Yeehats found in the forest, throats slashed. They begin to tell stories of a great Ghost Dog that runs at the head of the wolf pack. Buck's metamorphosis from civilized pet to legendary leader of the wilds is complete.

# THEMES

London incorporated two of his favorite ideologies in this story. Having read Darwin and Spencer, he believed in the evolution of the physical world and of society. In this story, both environment and society played important parts in determining Buck's behavior and future.

## Naturalism

In Naturalistic writing, everything happens in the physical realm and is explainable by observation of physical events. London skillfully uses nature to demonstrate how Buck adapts to his new environment. Functioning in the physical environment of the North requires certain skills. Buck must master these new skills not only to thrive, but to survive. For example, the bitter cold requires that Buck learn how to deal with ice between his toes and how to burrow in the snow for warmth at night. Buck is subject to the laws of physics. The sled must be properly loaded so it can be pulled without tipping over. He must figure out how to dislodge the sled from ice and how to get out of the way of the sled on a downhill run. With each new skill learned, Buck becomes less dependent upon man. Eventually, he is totally self-sufficient.

## Determinism

While Buck progresses in his survival skills, he regresses in his social skills. Buck's environment of masters and other dogs determines how he behaves. This concept that environment alone shapes a person is called determinism. London applies determinism to Buck to justify his moral regression. He uses Buck's interactions with his various masters and with other dogs and wolves to do this.

> **DETERMINISM**—*The belief that every idea and action is predetermined and cannot be changed; negating a person's free will.*

Buck's progression of experiences contrasts his intellectual and physical mastery with his moral decline. For example, the man with the red sweater is Buck's initiation into the "law of the club." He learns that a man with a club is superior to a dog, and man is no longer to be trusted. Buck learns the "law of fang" by watching other dogs devour Curly. This, too, puts him on his guard. These experiences awaken his instinct.

As Buck works for Perrault and Francois, he builds stamina and strength as he toils for hours on end, day after day. He begins to master the relationships within the team. When a dog steals his meat, he studies their methods and becomes the best thief in the camp so that even Perrault does not suspect him. But he learns the most from Spitz. Spitz has instinct and cunning. As the two interact, Spitz is actually training Buck to be the leader. By the end of his stay with Perrault and Francois, Buck has become master of his society. He is superior in both cunning and physical strength.

The unhappy trio that buys Buck provides a nice contrast between those who cannot adapt to the environment and those who can. Their inability or refusal to adapt leads to death. Buck adapts quickly and completely, gaining superiority. Thornton serves a slightly different purpose. Buck's loving response to Thornton proves that even after Buck has completely regressed from his civilized life, he can be reclaimed by love.

London drives home his point on determinism in the last chapter. Buck returns each year to the place where Thornton was killed and pays him homage.

Buck's response to love is love. On the other hand, he continues to attack Yeehat hunters year after year. His response to violence is violence.

## The Dominant Primordial Beast

Buck masters three areas to prove his right to be the dominant primordial beast. First, he masters nature. He learns to live with hunger when there is no food, then to hunt for his own food in the wild. Second, he demonstrates mastery over his own kind. Not only does he kill the dominant Spitz, he takes Spitz's job as leader and outperforms him. He masters all other dogs, whether those on the team or any dog that threatens Thornton.

Lastly, Buck masters mankind. Once Buck is received into the hands of the dog traders, he feels fear for the first time. He learns to fear a man with a club when he meets the man in the red sweater. He develops cautious relationships with each new owner, respecting some and despising others. London makes clear that even though Buck learns to love Thornton, he still retains his hard-earned wilderness instincts. Buck finally masters mankind in the end when he meets the Yeehats in the valley of the miners. Even though the Indians have weapons, his love for Thornton enables him to surmount their advantage.

In his rage, Buck becomes fearless and kills even humans.

## Literary Devices

By using anthropomorphism (giving human traits to animals) London is able to demonstrate his theories of socialization to good effect. Buck's "de-evolution" into stealing and killing is far less shocking when viewed within the animal kingdom. Yet it only takes a small mental leap to apply the process to humans. One way London accomplishes this feat convincingly is by presenting the story from the dog's point of view. He uses "dog psychology,"[11] presenting the story by inferring the way a dog would think and act. He does this primarily through identifiable human emotions. Buck experiences jealousy and revenge toward Spitz. He demonstrates loyalty, love, and devotion for Thornton. He even shows patience in stalking a moose. Buck's emotions make the transition easier from dog story to human allegory.

A second technique of London's is to use basic needs to drive the changes in Buck. For example, hunger often drives Buck's regression. He first learns to steal through hunger. Hunger sharpens his instincts. Hunger fuels his bloodlust. Because hunger is a universal experience, the reader can rationalize or even excuse the regression—especially when Buck's hunger borders on starvation.

## The Making of a Hero

Buck's journey from civilization to the primitive follows the typical pattern of the mythical hero. The five general stages of development are a call to adventure, separation, initiation, transformation, and return.[12] As Buck moves through these stages, his moral development regresses while his instincts increase. His very survival depends upon denying his moral training.

The discovery of gold in the Yukon, though it does not involve Buck directly, serves as his call to adventure. Buck's separation occurs when he is taken from Judge Miller's ranch in California and transported to the North. Up to this point, Buck has learned to trust the people who are in his life. He has had no reason to develop his instincts. From this point of separation, Buck's fears begin to develop and become an integral part of his ability to survive.

Initiation occurs immediately afterward with two major incidents, the law of club—learned at the hand of the man with the red sweater; and the law of fang—learned as he watches Curly brutalized and killed by a pack of dogs. The initiation flows into a series of tests, demonstrating Buck's ability to adapt to his new environment, combining his civilized intellect and his primitive instincts.

During the hero cycle, a benevolent helper typically aids the hero during his transformation. In Buck's case, his early helpers are Perrault and Francois. They protect him from Spitz as he adapts to life in the wilderness. Once Buck develops his primordial skills, Thornton serves as his escort deep into the wilderness.

In a typical hero story, the hero returns to his point of origin, now stronger and equipped to benefit his fellow man. In *The Call of the Wild*, Buck's return is not to civilization, but to his more primitive, ancestral beginnings as a wild animal. London uses this twist on the hero's return to the primitive instead of the civilized as a nod to Darwin's theories.

## The Call of the Writer

In the same year that *The Call of the Wild* was published, 1903, London published eighteen stories and essays, and two more books, and he finished writing *The Sea-Wolf*. He had grown tired of the public's requests for more stories of the Northland and struck out in various directions. Even before *The Call of the Wild* came out, London began experimenting with different types of writing.

# BEYOND THE NORTHLAND

Over the course of his career, London wrote both fiction and nonfiction, including science fiction, children stories, socialist commentary/ propaganda, short stories, and news reporting. After writing *The Call of the Wild*, London accepted a job from the American Press Association to cover the end of the Boer Wars in South Africa. He took this job partly to escape his failing marriage but mostly to cover his three thousand dollars of debt. He stopped over in New York to see Brett, and while there he contracted with Macmillan to write a book on the condition of slums in London's East End during his layover in England. This arrangement was to London's advantage because his series of articles on the Boer Wars was cancelled and his ticket to England was already paid for.

# INTO THE ABYSS

The title of London's book, *The People of the Abyss,* came from H.G. Well's term for the urban poor.[1] London arrived in England, disguised himself as a down-and-out American sailor just arrived and went to live alongside the people he was reporting on. He experienced the horrors of urban civilization first hand and reported what he saw. His book was padded with charts and statistics from other sources, but the narrative sections reveal London's outrage at the living conditions of what was then the capitalist center of the Western world: "If this is the best that civilisation can do for the human, then give us howling and naked savagery. Far better to be a people of the wilderness and desert, of the cave and the squatting place, than to be a people of the machine and of the Abyss."[2]

London's reference to the wilderness puts his indignation in perspective. After witnessing the physical hardship of the natural environment in the Northland, he decided that man-made hardship created by industrialism was far worse. It fueled the fire of his socialism, moving him from passive protestor to revolutionary.

These feelings were probably intensified by London's own narrow escape from the Social Pit, as evidenced in his article "How I Became a Socialist."

Written just after his return from England, it reveals his deep-seated fear of falling back into the pit. This article indicates a schism in London's thinking that eventually leads him to resign from the Socialist Party just months before his death. Socialists generally identified with the working class and tried to improve their lives.

**SCHISM**—*A division with opposing sides.*

London, on the other hand, feared the working class life and wanted to escape from it.[3] He never overcame this fear, as evidenced in his California novels written toward the end of his career. In *The Valley of the Moon*, the main characters reject their lower-class existence in the city and go in search of an agrarian dream. These characters articulate in London's fiction what he only hints at in his article about becoming a socialist.

*The People of the Abyss* became very popular at home in the United States. Surprisingly, the book sold almost twenty million copies in America, making it profitable. In England, the reception was quite cool. Jack London had revealed the dirty part of industrialism in that country, and it was not taken kindly.[4]

**AGRARIAN**—*Relating to the land or agriculture.*

And although the book was not a socialist treatise on the poor, it brought Jack London to the forefront of the socialist movement.

**75**

# THE KEMPTON–WACE LETTERS

Another of London's early attempts to draw away from the Northland stories was coauthored with his friend and love interest Anna Strunsky. London met Strunkstry in 1899 at some of the socialist meetings he attended. London was attracted to Strunsky but suddenly decided to marry Bessie Maddern, a woman who fit his ideal for a mother for his desired Anglo-Saxon progeny.

After his marriage, London continued his friendship with Strunsky. Anna was a materialist intellectually but an idealist at heart. She could not decide whether it was better to marry for practical reasons or for reasons of the heart. London proposed that they settle the matter through a series a letters,

**MATERIALIST**—*One who believes that the physical world is the only reality, and all things can be explained in those terms.*

with him taking the side of logic and science, and with her taking the side of the romantic idealist. The result was a series of letters collected into a book called the *Kempton–Wace Letters.* When London stopped by New York on his way to England, Brett agreed to publish the letters using pseudonyms so as not to distract from the upcoming marketing push for *The Call of the Wild.*

Strunsky, using the pseudonym Dane Kempton, tries to convince the younger Wace that romantic love is not only necessary for marriage, but also desirable. London, writing as Herbert Wace, masterfully presents his arguments for foregoing romance for the sake of science. Wace's arguments support London's belief that the best way to produce a superior race is through selective breeding.

Ironically, London had chosen his first wife, Bessie Maddern, based on this ideal. While he was writing this book, his own marriage was falling apart. His disillusionment with his scientific ideal became evident when he allowed the Kempton character's ideas to win out in the book. London's experiment with marrying for breeding purposes was a failure.

# THE RUSSO–JAPANESE WAR

London twice took on the job of war correspondent. The first time, in 1904, he accepted a job from the Hearst Syndicate to report on the Russo–Japanese War. The Japanese and Russians were fighting for control over Manchuria. London arrived in Tokyo, only to find that the journalists were

**HEARST SYNDICATE—** *Newspaper operation owned by William Randolph Hearst.*

idle, waiting for permission from the Japanese government to go to the front to report on the war.

**RUSSO–JAPANESE WAR**—*Military conflict between Japan and Russia over the province of Manchuria, taking place from 1904 to 1905.*

London, forever the adventurer and tired of waiting, set out on his own for Manchuria via Korea. Upon landing in Korea, he was arrested for being a Russian spy. After the local officials were convinced he was just an American journalist, he was let go. He had two more arrests, the second of which amounted to an international incident. Richard Harding Davis, a famous American journalist, intervened on London's behalf by wiring President Roosevelt about the problem. Roosevelt contacted the Japanese and London was released, with the stipulation that he return home immediately. He complied.

Because the Japanese government hindered the efforts of all reporters, London's war coverage was minimal. He witnessed one battle between the

**YELLOW PERIL**—*In late 1800s, the fear that Chinese and Japanese immigration would lower the value of the American worker. The phrase was used prominently in newspapers in the Hearst Syndicate.*

Russians and Japanese. Most of his stories covered his own experiences, detailing his exploits and the condition of the two armies he observed. London had no love for the Japanese. In his reporting, London sided with

Jack London spent three months living among the poor of London's East End in 1902 in order to research his book, *The People of the Abyss.*

the Russians. He was very much against the so-called "yellow peril" of the oriental races. He believed that the Japanese should be subjugated to the Russians. Although he admired their military discipline, he did not appreciate their culture. His tendency toward impulsive action clashed with the Japanese culture of subtlety and pauses to ponder significance of actions.

When he returned to the United States, London voiced his opinions about his experiences in his socialist meetings. His comrades were flabbergasted that he would lambaste the Japanese race as a whole. The socialists were interested in the working class, regardless of race. London's comments, which amounted to racial prejudice, revealed a darker side to the man. When some of his comrades tried to point out his un-socialist thinking he responded with, "I am first of all a white man and only then a socialist!"[5] Because many of his views were inconsistent with those of the socialist movement, some began to consider him a liability to the cause even though he still received invitations to speak at socialist events.

# THE MEXICAN REVOLUTION

Again in 1914, London took on the job of correspondent during the Mexican Revolution. This time, he worked for *Collier's* for fourteen hundred dollars a week. In 1910 at the beginning of the conflict, London was against the United States' intervention in the conflict. His short story "The Mexican" is a sympathetic portrait of a Mexican boxer who bests his gringo opponent, using the prize money to buy arms for the revolution.

**MEXICAN REVOLUTION**—*A violent political upheaval in Mexico beginning in 1910 and lasting until the latter 1920s. It began as an armed uprising against the government but became a series of power struggles as different factions within the country fought for control of Mexico.*

By the time London went to Mexico in 1914, his attitude had changed dramatically. For example, he now sided with U.S. intervention, which was led by capitalists wanting to exploit the oil fields of Mexico. Second, he no longer spouted the rhetoric of socialism. He spoke out against the common laborer—the very people socialists supported. Living the bourgeois life of riches and travel and owning the ranch made him into a practicing capitalist, even if he still claimed socialist leanings. His articles from this adventure served to discredit him among socialists, journalists, and the general public.[6]

As in the Klondike and the South Seas, London had to cut his adventure short due to health problems. London left the war zone because of an acute attack of dysentery.

## SURPRISE AT HOME

In the midst of his work as a war correspondent, London's personal life was in choas. Upon his return from covering the Russo-Japanese War in 1904, Bessie filed for divorce claiming extreme cruelty. She strongly suspected London was having an affair. She named Anna Strunsky as his love interest in the divorce papers due to their close association in writing The Kempton–Wace Letters. The media got hold of this information and reported it. Anna Strunsky publicly declared she was not involved with Jack London, even though he had proposed marriage to her before he left for England. Bessie confided her troubles to Charmian Kitteredge, the woman who, ironically, should have been named in the divorce papers. London and Charmian had kept their affair secret even from their closest friends. When Bessie found out the truth, she never forgave Charmian for pretending concern over London's straying.

London's next novel, *The Sea-Wolf*, gives clues about his involvement with and appreciation for Charmian. The sole female character shows up half way through the story, about the same time London became involved with Charmian. The love story in the book reflects his feelings for her at that time. He now obviously believed wholeheartedly in Dane Kempton's point of view about love.

# A LOVE STORY

**W**ith *The Sea-Wolf* (1904), London looked back to his experience aboard the *Sophie Sutherland* when he was seventeen. Brett thought the timing for a sea story was very good because there were not very many out in the marketplace at that time. London took his small sailboat, the *Spray*, and sailed around his old haunts to re-familiarize himself with sea life.

## PLOT SUMMARY

Humphrey Van Weyden, Dean of American Letters, is on a ferryboat in San Francisco Bay when it capsizes in a collision in the fog. Van Weyden passes out during the rescue effort and begins floating out to sea. A sealing schooner, captained by the nefarious Wolf Larsen, picks him up. Larsen is a brutal sea captain, running a ship that functions as a miniature society where might is right and life has no value.

Van Weyden tries to negotiate a return to San Francisco, but Larsen happens to be one man short on his boat and decides to keep Van Weyden aboard the *Ghost* on a whim. He determines that Van Weyden has stood "on dead men's legs"[1] for too long, referring to his being a gentlemen and living solely off his inheritance. Larsen wants to see him work for a living. He believes he is doing Van Weyden a favor by helping him become a man. Humphrey Van Weyden, reduced to the name Hump, is assigned the position of cabin boy. From his newly lowered social vantage point, Hump both witnesses and experiences the brutality that runs rampant on the ship. In this microcosm of society on the sea, evil for evil is the maxim.

Larsen is an enigma to Hump. One day while cleaning Larsen's stateroom, Hump finds a library consisting of Shakespeare, Poe, and Darwin, among others. Hump cannot immediately reconcile the brutal lord of the ship with the learned volumes he finds. Just before reaching the seal hunting grounds, Larsen begins to experience severe headaches, causing him to retreat to his stateroom for days at a time. When they reach the seal hunting grounds, they encounter Wolf's brother, Death Larsen. The Larsen brothers are similar in all things except one. Death Larsen is barely literate. He has not widened his world through his mind. He functions only on instinct and will.

Various members of the *Ghost*'s crew try to escape the ship while out seal hunting, only to be caught and punished severely. One day while out looking for two seamen who ran off during a heavy fog, the *Ghost* comes across a boat with five people in it—four men and a woman. The woman is none other than Maud Brewster, an American poet known by name to Van Weyden, on her way to Japan to recover her health. Van Weyden quickly falls in love with her, as does Larsen.

Tension grows and distrust mounts as the sole woman on board ship attracts the ship's captain and Hump, now the ship's first mate. Van Weyden's distrust in Larsen proves well founded when he awakens one night to find Larsen attacking Maud. He quickly intervenes, knowing that this act could be his last. In the middle of the scuffle, Larsen has one of his headache attacks and can no longer fight. Van Weyden helps him into bed, then he and Maud escape on a well-equipped sealing boat. Through cold, rain, and wind, they labor on through the sea until they land on a small, uncharted island.

Living on the island, they resign themselves to a stay of months, possibly even years, while they wait for rescue. They spend weeks building a shelter (with two separate rooms for propriety's sake for the Victorian audience) and stocking it with wood and food for the winter. Throughout this time, they grow in mutual respect for each other. Van Weyden bears the fruit of his newfound masculinity and Maud is an invaluable help to Van Weyden, helping with chores he could never do alone.

Their romantic interlude is interrupted the morning they find the *Ghost* floating in the cove they call home. Van Weyden investigates and finds that the ship has been abandoned, all except for Wolf Larsen. The crew has gone over to Death Larsen's ship, but not before damaging the masts and sails. In addition, Wolf Larsen's headaches have gotten so bad that he is now blind and in pain much of the time.

Van Weyden decides to repair the *Ghost* and sail it back to waters where they are likely to meet other boats. Upon finishing the repairs, Van Weyden and Maud sail off into the sunset. Larsen suffers another series of strokes and dies shortly after they set sail. They give him a burial at sea just as they sight another boat to rescue them. The story ends with Maud calling Van Weyden her man, and Van Weyden calling Maud "his one small woman."[2]

## THEMES

There are several themes working throughout this story. The most obvious theme is the one espoused by Larsen: might is right. Larsen feels justified in doing what he does simply because he is the strongest. Wrapped within this theme of might is right is the idea that there is no inherent value to life. This theme can be traced to London's view of Darwinism. Darwinism implies that individual lives are not as important as propagation of the species; therefore life only has value as far as it can make the species stronger. The death of weak individuals is not only logical but is expected and even desirable.

Larsen obviously holds to this same view, but he cannot reconcile it with the will to live. In Larsen's view, life is only valuable to the person living it. He declares that even though a life is worthless, the will to live remains strong. Here, London uses Nietzsche's idea of the will-to-power and plays it against the instinctual will-to-live. However, London was not really true to Nietzsche's ideas because "London, like other Americans, mangled Nietzsche, who insisted man must conquer the inner beast in his search for power, not unleash its reckless and destructive powers."[3] Larsen uses his will-to-power destructively. For example, Larsen, in his typically sadistic way, nearly chokes Van Weyden to death. When Van Weyden resists, Larsen proves that

**FREDERICH NIETZSCHE—** *German philosopher most famous for his line, "God is dead." He promoted the idea of a "will to power" as humankind's most fundamental drive.*

Van Weyden's will-to-live is stronger than his willingness to die.

Another minor theme is that of courage. Throughout the story, Van Weyden finds himself growing in courage. His soft life as a scholar has given him no opportunity to develop courage. In contrast, each encounter on board the *Ghost* gives him the chance to grow stronger—both physically and mentally. Van Weyden's greatest revelation comes when he sees that Wolf Larsen is truly fearless. Van Weyden realizes that because Larsen has no fears, he has no true courage. London uses this realization to separate the two men: Larsen is one-dimensional in his power; he is all about brute strength. Van Weyden, on the other hand, tempers his courage with idealism. Van Weyden has become a man while Larsen remains like an animal.

# Plot Development

London's handling of the plot takes some surprising turns. He starts out creating what has been called one of American literature's most memorable characters in Wolf Larsen, but then introduces a main character halfway through the book. At that point, he turns a story of high adventure into a Victorian romance. Many critics at the time thought the introduction of Maud Brewster at the halfway point was bad plotting. However, London stated that he used the presence of the woman to prove Van Weyden's newly acquired manhood. Larsen was the foil against which he earned his manhood while Maud was the foil against which he proved it.

Modern critics delve deeper and examine the roles of male and female in this work. In the beginning Van Weyden is described as effeminate. He has to earn his manhood on the high seas. Maud is the era's New Woman. Although frail, she does a man's work when they escape, but she remains completely feminine. By the end of the story, both Van Weyden and Maud have achieved a sort of androgyny.[4] They are clearly male and female, but both

**ANDROGYNY**—*A blending of both male and female characteristics.*

exhibit characteristics of the opposite sex. Viewed in light of London's recent affair with Charmian, this showed his appreciation for her similar characteristics. At the same time, he challenged society's view of the masculine and feminine.

# CHARACTER DEVELOPMENT

*The Sea-Wolf* follows one of London's favorite themes—the initiation story. Van Weyden's dunking in the bay serves as his baptism and rebirth into his new life aboard the *Ghost*. The novel is structured so that Larsen starts out strong and declines throughout the story while Van Weyden begins weak and becomes strong.[5] As the story progresses, Larsen begins to decline due to his headaches and neurological problems, the unsuccessful mutiny of the crew, and the appearance of his brother Death Larsen, who is more evil and brutal than he is.

While Larsen is declining in power and strength, Van Weyden is learning how to be a man in a man's world. He learns how to work for a living, how to defend himself against evil, and how to overcome his fears. The crossover point occurs when Larsen accosts Maud Brewster and Van Weyden comes to her defense. From that point forward, Van Weyden gains the superior position.

This interplay between duality and reversal is yet another of London's favorite techniques. In *The Sea-Wolf*, London may have tried to cram too much into a single story. He was much more successful with duality and reversal when he used two completely different stories to make his points, such as in *The Call of the Wild* and *White Fang*.

## PERSONAL LIFE

London rushed *The Sea-Wolf* to completion by the end of 1903. He also separated from Bessie at this time.

It took two years for his divorce to become final. On November 19, 1905, he married his new love, Charmian Kitteredge, while on a tour of the United States giving talks on socialism. Marrying her so abruptly after his divorce was shocking and offensive to many people. For a time, it adversely affected his career and public image.

*The Sea-Wolf* was London's second most popular book until 1906, when *White Fang* surpassed it in popularity and sales. As with *The Call of the Wild*, London used animals to tell his story.

# THE OTHER DOG STORY

**W**hite Fang was a deliberate attempt by London to reverse the process he described in *The Call of the Wild*. In 1902 London told Brett, "I'm going to give the evolution, the civilisation of a dog—development of domesticity, faithfulness, love, morality."[1] Although *White Fang* was never as popular as *The Call of the Wild*, the public received it well. The book sold enough copies to make a healthy profit for Macmillan.

## PLOT SUMMARY

### Part 1—The Wild

Two men, Bill and Henry, traveling through the frozen Northland are being tracked by a pack of hungry wolves. There is a she-wolf among them that is half dog. Over time, she lures the men's sled dogs away, until Bill decides to go after her with a shotgun. Henry stays back, watching and listening to the pursuit. He hears three shots, a cry, and then no more. The wolves have devoured Bill and the last of the dogs.

Henry spends the night alone, staying awake near the fire to keep the wolves at bay. Each night thereafter, the wolves become more desperate, closing in on Henry in spite of the fire. He finally ends up building a circle of fire around himself to keep the wolves away. As that fire burns out, the wolves approach. He sits in the circle of dying flames and goes to sleep, knowing that the wolves have won. Instead, he awakens to silence. The appearance of a group of men has scared the wolves away.

## Part 2—Born of the Wild

The she-wolf who runs with the pack mates with one of the leaders, giving birth to a litter of five pups. A time of famine comes and all the pups die except one. This one has a wolf's coloring, a dog's intelligence, and the stamina of a strong, wild wolf. The pup's first lesson is on hunting. He quickly learns, "The aim of life was meat . . . There were the eaters and the eaten. The law was: EAT OR BE EATEN."[2]

One day, in the midst of the famine, a lynx invades their lair and attacks the mother. When the lynx brings the mother down, the pup joins the attack and the two of them kill the lynx. Although the mother is seriously wounded, she recovers and they begin to go out together to hunt for food.

## Part 3—The Gods of the Wild

One day near the lair, the pup comes across a new type of living thing—a "man-god." White Fang goes to live in the Indian camp with the one named Gray Beaver. He learns the laws of living with humans and with those of his own kind. Through several beatings, each more severe than the last, he learns that his man-god, Gray Beaver, is to be obeyed at all times. The other pups take the lead of Lip-Lip, the dominant pup, and torment White Fang. White Fang becomes a ferocious fighter and a loner. Because of this shunning, "he never knew a moment's security. The tooth of every dog was against him, and the hand of every man."[3]

## Part 4—The Superior Gods

During the early part of the Klondike gold rush, Gray Beaver goes into the town of Dawson to trade his furs. White Fang, with his distinctive wolf coloring, attracts a lot of attention. One onlooker in particular, Beauty Smith, decides he must own White Fang. Since he knows "the ways of Indians,"[4] he befriends

Gray Beaver, giving him a gift of whiskey, then sells him bottle after bottle. Soon, Gray Beaver is indebted to Smith and hands over White Fang.

Beauty Smith is an evil man filled with evil ways. Smith beats White Fang, leaves him tied up all day, and eventually cages him. Smith puts him on public display where people point at him and poke him with sticks to see his vicious reaction. White Fang learns hostility and hatred. Smith plans to make money off White Fang by entering him into dogfights.

White Fang, now known as "The Fighting Wolf," bests all dogs he fights. He even fights two dogs at once, and a lynx at another time. He beats them all until the day he is faced with a bulldog. They enter into a protracted fight to the death. This fight is almost at an end when Weedon Scott, a local mining expert from a nearby claim, splits the dogs apart and buys an all-but-dead White Fang to save him from Smith. White Fang has never known love and takes a while to warm up to Scott. In the end, love prevails and White Fang gives his allegiance to Scott.

## Part 5—The Tame

The time comes when Weedon Scott must return home to California. Scott takes White Fang home to his father's estate. White Fang must learn yet a new set of rules for life in the Southland. He learns to tolerate Scott's children, to get along with the dogs on the estate, and to overcome his strong instincts to chase the chickens and other animals on the ranch.

One day an escaped convict, Jim Hall, comes to seek revenge on Judge Scott for sentencing him to prison for a crime he did not commit. As Jim Hall gains the stairway in the entrance hall, White Fang attacks. Man and beast fight it out with gun and fang. By the time Scott and his father make it downstairs, Jim Hall is dead and White Fang is almost dead. The veterinarian gives White Fang a one-in-a-thousand chance of survival. White Fang beats the odds and goes on to father a litter of pups.

# A Lesson in Determinism

*White Fang* functions as a fable, with the moral lesson that society makes the man. London preaches environmental determinism throughout the story, often through direct statements from the narrator. For example, the two reprobates in the story, Beauty Smith and Jim Hall, are both described as short-changed by nature in their physical make-up and the people around them treat them evilly. Therefore, London asserts, they are not responsible for being the way they are: brutal and unloving toward man and beast. London makes similar statements about White Fang, attributing his changes to those around him.

By using a dog as the main character, London takes the emphasis on environment one step further. Dogs in the real world are subject to their owners. Likewise, White Fang is never free to make his own decisions or create his own reality. His circumstances are dictated by his man-god. Free will—which is nonexistent in the purest form of determinism— is severely limited. He is forced into the role of responder. His character is predicated upon the environment around him, especially the treatment he receives from others. When beaten into submission, he is submissive. When lovingly handled by Scott, he is loving.

## SETTING

Setting plays a major part in demonstrating the effects of environment on White Fang. In each part of the story, the setting is less wild and more civilized. Initially, White Fang's mother is shown totally in the wild, even though she has obviously had domestication in her life at some point. Part two shows White Fang living in the wilderness and learning to hunt for his food. He is a wild thing learning the laws of the wild—hunting for his own food and fighting his own fights.

Part three moves White Fang into an Indian camp where White Fang learns to live with men and with those of his own kind. Fourth, White Fang moves to the town of Dawson, learning how to live with a multitude of men in a closer setting. By Part Five, White Fang goes to live in the country on Judge Scott's estate. By moving White Fang around so much, London shows the various levels of society White Fang must master in order to become civilized.

## CHARACTER DEVELOPMENT

Throughout the story, there is a dual conflict going on. Externally, the conflict flares between White Fang and society. He is hated by man and beast alike during his stay in the Indian camp. His instinctive response is to fight back and dominate. But when he does, Gray Beaver beats him into submission. He begins to overcome instinct in order to function in the human world. This sets up the second conflict: White Fang versus himself, or his inner nature. London uses these two conflicts to highlight the interplay of instinct and intellect during White Fang's domestication.

With each change of setting, White Fang learns more about how to live among men. He learns to assert reason over instinct, displaying a new level of self-control with each change of ownership. With Beauty Smith, his control comes from hatred. By the time he meets Scott, his instinctual fighting response is well under control but he still has one more step to take. He needs to learn to control himself out of love, not fear. The proof of this love comes when White Fang defends the judge's family from attack, even though he suffers near-fatal wounds. With this sacrifice, his metamorphosis is complete.

## COMPARISON TO *THE CALL OF THE WILD*

In order to achieve his complete reversal of the de-civilizing process described in *The Call of the Wild*, London uses a lot of the same settings and character types. *Call* starts on a California estate, moves to the city and eventually to deep in the wilds. *White Fang* starts in the wild, moves to the city, then to a country estate in California. Both Buck and White Fang meet inept owners, indifferent owners, and those who show love. Buck's owners escort him from civilization to the wild. White Fang's owners introduce him slowly but surely to civilization.

London chose different genres and underlying philosophies for these two tales. Whereas *Call* is a hero story, *White Fang* is a fable. The first tells a tale; the second makes a point. The hero story is told in the context of naturalism; the fable in the context of determinism. Buck reverts to a natural, instinctual existence; White Fang conquers instinct to become civilized.

Both stories emphasize the need to adapt in order to survive. Buck's entry into the rugged wilderness requires the same level of adaptability for survival as White Fang's entry into civilization. Both dogs are shaped by adversity, and their ultimate success depends on fully developing both intellect and instinct.

## THE NATURE FAKIR

*White Fang*'s popularity was helped along when the president, Theodore Roosevelt, read it and called London and other writers "nature fakirs." Nature fakirs falsify the natural world in order to make a point or further an agenda. Roosevelt admitted that his comments were unusual for a President, but he felt compelled to point out the unrealistic representation of animal behavior in London's novel, especially the besting of a wolf by a bulldog—the pivotal fight during White Fang's tenure as The Fighting Wolf. Roosevelt's comments appeared in an article in

*Everybody's Magazine*. London responded in *Collier's*, claiming freedom of literary license.

The president was not alone in his criticism. Many experts familiar with wolves decried London's descriptions of interactions between wolves and humans. Wolves are typically terrified of humans and only attack in extreme cases of hunger. However, the reading public either did not notice or did not care. They bought the story as a true representation of animal behavior. London helped perpetuate the still-common myth of the mighty, attacking wolf.

## MOVING ON

Like White Fang, London made a move from the Northland to southern climes in his writing. In real life, he embarked on a world cruise aboard his boat the *Snark*. His first stop was Hawaii. He would then sail on to the South Seas.

# THE
# SNARK

L ondon's boat was named after the creature in Lewis Carroll's tale *The Hunting of the Snark: An Agony in Eight Fits*. The story of that ill-fated cruise was but a harbinger of things to come for London's *Snark*.

London wrote his book, *The Cruise of the Snark*, to make money to pay for the trip and the continuing work at the ranch. It is filled with slice-of-life stories about the trip and has the feel of a romance novel. London's cook on the voyage, Martin Johnson, wrote his own book several years later titled *Through the South Seas with Jack London* (1913). This book is quite different. It reads more like a documentary, with personal details from his diary and bits of history thrown in. The two books, when read together, tell a more complete story of London's trip through the South Seas.

## TRAVELOGUE

About four years before the trip began, the Londons had read Joshua Slocum's *Sailing Alone Around the*

*World.* Slocum made the trip in a thirty-five-foot boat, taking three years to complete the journey. The Londons began to think about the possibilities of doing the same thing. They soon decided that they could do it together in a forty-five-foot boat. They planned a seven-year voyage that began in San Francisco and went to Hawaii, the South Seas, the Far East, around Africa, to Europe, then back to America, cutting across the continent on various rivers and canals. The boat was designed to sail the high seas and to navigate through rivers so they could explore inland along rivers like the Seine (France) and the Rhine (Germany).

The building of the boat was a catastrophe. The cost, estimated at seven thousand dollars (Slocum's cost him less than six hundred dollars), went up to thirty thousand. London could have bought a similar boat for well under ten thousand but he wanted the satisfaction of building it himself. As he explains in the foreward of *The Cruise of the Snark,* "The thing I like most of all is personal achievement—not achievement for the world's applause, but achievement for my own delight. It is the old 'I did it! I did it! With my own hands I did it!'"[1]

In order to pay for the boat and to continue running the ranch in his absence, he contracted with various magazines and book publishers for stories

Jack London greatly enjoyed spending time aboard his boat and taking sea trips.

related to the trip. When the *Snark* left the dock in San Francisco, it was barely seaworthy. London decided to sail it to Hawaii and make repairs there—away from the media and his friends, who had been taking bets on his departure date for months beforehand. The Londons and their crew made it in twenty-seven days, although the newspapers had already published accounts stating they were lost at sea.

After several months of repairs, the *Snark* was ready to return to the sea. From Hawaii, it traveled to the South Seas, visiting Tahiti, Typee, the Fiji Islands, and the Solomon Islands. Eventually, the entire crew came down with various tropical diseases. The Londons moved on to Australia to seek medical care. There, London decided to abandon the trip. Although both grieved the loss of their great adventure, Charmian felt the loss most keenly. London said, "In hospital when I broke the news to Charmian that I must go back to California, the tears welled into her eyes. For two days she was wrecked and broken by the knowledge that the happy, happy, voyage was abandoned."[2] Before leaving Australia, London sold the *Snark* for a mere three thousand dollars.

# HAWAII

Although Hawaii did not become a state until 1959, the Hawaiian government had ceded the "Kingdom of Hawaii" to the U.S. government in 1889, giving the U.S. government complete sovereignty over the nation. The islanders were multicultural, with Americans, native islanders, Japanese, and Chinese living there. While repairs were made to the *Snark*, Jack and Charmian toured the islands and were the guests of many of Hawaii's elite. They socialized with dignitaries and commercial barons. They climbed the peaks of Hawaii's volcanoes. But when they spent their Fourth of July on the island of Molokai at a colony for people with leprosy, they ran into resistance from the upper classes.

London wrote several stories featuring Hawaii. One of his most famous is "Koolau the Leper." In this story, a small group of lepers on the island of Kauai has banded together to resist deportation to Molokai and the leper colony. They retreat to a small paradise high in the mountains and take a stand. After many are killed

**LEPROSY**—*A chronic disease of the skin, flesh, and nerves resulting in ulcers, scaly skin, and deformities caused by nerve damage.*

and the rest surrender, Koolau alone remains on the run from the army. He fends them off with his Mauser gun, pulling the trigger with the joint on his thumb—the last digit left that can work the trigger. The army chases him for six weeks, then finally leaves him in peace. Koolau lives another two years, killing those who seek him, but only in self-defense.

When he senses his life is at its end, he crawls into a thicket to die. He had achieved his goal of dying a free man rather than a prisoner of Molokai. London masterfully paints the poignant scene of Koolau's final moments:

> His eyelids fluttered wearily down and the drip of the rain ceased in his ears. A prolonged trembling set up in his body. This, too, ceased. He half-lifted his head, but it fell back. Then his eyes opened, and did not close. His last thought was of his Mauser, and he pressed it against his chest with his folded, fingerless hands. So passed Koolau, the leper.

Two other short stories, "The Sheriff of Kona" and "Good-bye, Jack" also reveal the plight of the leper in the islands. In his fictional stories, the colony on Molokai is painted as it was in its earliest days—as a last resort prison for people afflicted with leprosy. Yet in his nonfiction book *The Cruise of the Snark*, London paints a picture of the Molokai he saw—a paradise for lepers cast out by society but living happily.

## THE MESSAGE

When London reverts to using the earlier conditions of the leper colony in his stories, he is not just adding dramatic tension. He is a making a blatant political statement. Although probably not obvious to the average American reader of the time, it was painfully obvious to the Hawaiian elite who had just entertained the Londons in high fashion.

For example, in "Koolau the Leper," the conflict seems to be man against man, at least on the surface. Digging a little deeper, the conflict is really about man versus society. London makes his political statement in the opening lines spoken by Koolau: "Because we are sick they take away our liberty. We have obeyed the law. We have done no wrong. And yet they would put us in prison."[3] After giving the history of the invasion of the white imperialists—making no distinction between the missionaries and the merchants—he goes on to say, "They live like kings in houses of many rooms, with multitudes of servants to care for them. They who had nothing have everything. . . ."[4]

Adding insult to injury, London points out through Koolau that the disease they now suffer came from the Chinese slaves, brought there by white imperialists. The inhabitants who once lived peacefully on the islands were now subject to another race and the laws they made. Koolau realizes his stand against the imperialists will not win the war, but it will preserve his personal dignity.

## THE RESPONSE

After these stories were published, London's books were removed from bookstores and libraries in Hawaii for a time. London, demonstrating sympathy for the lepers, incited the wrath of the Hawaiian elite who had shown him such generous hospitality. By using leprosy as a "backdrop for the struggle against imperialism,"[5] he portrays the islanders as unsympathetic to both  the physical plight of the lepers and the social plight of the native islanders. London heightens the effect by playing on the public's natural fear of leprosy, often giving his characters extreme cases. Not all lepers rotted away to the grotesque figures that he describes.

Whether viewed as entertainment or political statement, London's use of the earlier, squalid conditions of the colony shows his mastery of reading the market, then romanticizing his experiences for his readers. London, as usual when confronted about his stories, pointed out that they were simply works of fiction. He always felt justified using fictional techniques to highlight the problems with the real world around him.

## THE SOLOMONS

In London's stories of the North, nature is a fierce foe, but it can be understood by those with imagination and it brings out the best in those who adapt to its harshness. In the South Seas, nature is chaotic and brings out the worst in man. London's negative view of the South Sea Islands was probably the result of the tropical diseases that he and his crew suffered there. These diseases eventually cut short his proposed trip around the world in the *Snark*.

London chose to portray white imperialists at their worst, rotting away under the effects of heat, disease, and alcohol. He chose to portray the Solomon Island natives at their worst, too—cannibals who measured success in the number of heads they collected, especially those of white men. In many of his South Seas stories, human suffering abounds, whether that of the white man or native. When physical health declines, man's morals deteriorate as well. In London's writing, white men in this lowered condition resort to cruelty toward the natives in an exercise of their supremacy. The natives respond with counterattacks and rebellion.

London once again supports the underdog. Even though he accepted Anglo-Saxon superiority as fact, he did not believe in mindless oppression of those conquered. He uses irony to point out the folly of those whose philosophy does include it. A good example of the interplay of oppressed and oppressor is found in his short story "Mauki."

In this story, London creates the character Bunster, a demented white man who delights in cowardly acts of brutality. He acquires a slave, Mauki, who puts up with Bunster's acts of violence, constantly looking for a way to retaliate. Mauki bides his time, and the time comes. Bunster falls ill of a fever. Mauki cares for him throughout, but when Bunster is past the fever and still weak, Mauki takes his revenge. He uses a ray skin glove of Bunster's that scrapes the skin off at a single swipe. Bunster has used this glove on many of the islanders, but mainly on Mauki. Mauki proceeds to skin Bunster alive, leaving him to die. Mauki then goes out to load his boat. London describes the final, grotesque scene: "It was while engaged in this that a hideous, skinless thing came out of the house and ran screaming down the beach till it fell in the sand and mewed and gibbered under the scorching sun. Mauki looked toward it and hesitated. Then he went over and removed the head, which he wrapped in a mat and stowed in the stern-locker of the cutter."[6] London uses irony to illustrate white supremacy gone very wrong. Bunster's moral callousness has been repaid "by having his thick hide removed entirely, and his sadistic head has become the trophy of its principal victim."[7]

# PUBLICITY

The entire trip of the *Snark* was of great interest to magazines and newspapers alike. Jack London's lifestyle lent itself to high drama and was therefore newsworthy. This trip was no exception. The media followed it with avid interest. London kept this interest alive by continuing to produce books and by writing for magazines so his stories continued to appear in print as he traveled.

Even on the cruise and in Hawaii, London wrote his one thousand words a day. He had to keep writing to fund his trip and the ranch back home. He completed two novels. One, *The Iron Heel*, was a futuristic tale of a socialist overthrow of the government. It was not much of a success with the public or with socialists. His other novel, *Martin Eden*, was written during the early part of the voyage.

# TRUE-
# LIFE
# WRITINGS

L ondon wrote two novels that reveal much about the man behind the hype. The first, *Martin Eden* (1909), tells the fictional tale of a seaman who, in three short years, becomes a phenomenally successful writer. It has many autobiographical elements related to London's rise to fame and his rise above the working class. Although critics at the time derided this meteoric rise as unrealistic, Jack London claimed, "I was Martin Eden."[1] The second book, *John Barleycorn*, is subtitled *Alcoholic Memoirs*, and it details London's life-long struggle with alcohol.

## MARTIN EDEN

As the story opens, Martin Eden is entering the home of a middle-class young man whom he has rescued from a fight on the docks. Although he feels very out of place, the man's sister, Ruth, enchants him. The family accepts him in their home and he determines to better himself through education. Ruth, who is falling in love with Eden even though she does not realize it, decides to help Eden in his self-improvement venture. Like Professor Higgins with Eliza Doolittle, Ruth attempts to mold Eden into the man that she would like him to be. And like Eliza Doolittle, Martin Eden has feelings and ideas of his own that do not mesh with Ruth's plans.

As Eden begins to show dramatic improvement, Ruth encourages him to find suitable work, even suggesting a place of employment for him. However, Eden wants to become a writer. He forsakes the sea and ignores Ruth's suggestions. He rents a room from a Portuguese woman, becoming the stereotypical starving artist—literally on the edge of starvation. He allows himself only five hours of sleep a night, and he repeatedly pawns his belongings to keep writing, then buys them back when he gets paid for his work. Ruth, growing frustrated with his lack of success and refusal to go a more conventional route, rejects him.

During this time in the gutter, Eden meets a man named Brissenden. This gentleman comes and goes, buying dinners occasionally for the starving Eden, and introduces him to the socialist movement in the Bay area. For the first time in his life, Eden has to defend what he believes. He thrives in this intellectually challenging environment, although he never really pursues it apart from Brissenden.

In the meantime, Eden sends out manuscript after manuscript, but most of them are returned. One day, he finally gets a big break. From that point forward, he is never in need of cash and never writes anything new. He simply resends out all the old writing that was originally rejected by the same publishers who are now eager for anything he has to sell.

His success assured, Ruth returns on the eve of an ocean voyage Eden is about to take to escape what his life has become. Ruth asks Eden to forgive her and take her back. Eden refuses. He leaves for his trip, only to slip through the porthole of his stateroom during the voyage to end his misery.

## LITERARY MERIT

The story functions as a *Bildungsroman*, a novel of the education or personal development of an individual. This education usually happens within the context of a specific social order, while the "student" moves from innocence to (a usually unhappy) knowledge. Martin Eden goes from a state of intellectual innocence as a working-class seaman to an unhappy knowledge of middle-class success.

In the early part of the novel, Eden's desire to know is fueled by his feelings for Ruth and his ambition.

**BILDUNGSROMAN—**
*A novel dealing with the education or development of a young protagonist, who then takes his place in society as a mature or knowledgeable adult.*

Ruth's rejection of his writing leads to emotional pain. The seemingly random acceptance of his writing leads to disillusionment. Both the fickle love of Ruth and the pinnacle of success—his two trophies for achieving middle-class status—leave him empty. The last lines of the book, spoken as he is drowning, sum up his discovery: "And somewhere at the bottom, he fell into darkness. That much he knew. He had fallen into darkness. And at the instant he knew, he ceased to know."[2] His education is complete.

The critical response to *Martin Eden* was less than enthusiastic. London had attempted the book as a condemnation of individualism. Instead, it appeared that London was promoting it through Eden's actions. The popular response was more positive.

# AUTOBIOGRAPHICAL MERIT

A Bildungsroman often contains autobiographical elements. There are many parallels between London and Eden. The most telling of these is their common view of the social classes. Like London, Eden begins in the lower class. Both long to rise above it; both choose to do so through writing. Both experience a meteoric rise to fame.

Two of the main characters are modeled after people that London knew well. The first, Ruth Morton, is modeled after London's first love Mabel Applegarth. The Applegarth family provided his introduction into middle-class society. Initially, London is impressed by Mabel's beauty and position, but he eventually comes to the conclusion that all women (or most of them, anyway) are really the same underneath, whether high born or low born. The other character, Brissenden, closely resembles London's friend, the poet George Sterling. Both are poets, both have socialist leanings, and each has become a sounding board for his literary friend.

The primary autobiographical merit comes from studying Eden's life and thought processes as he goes through the change from seaman to writer, from the working class to the middle class. For example, Eden pursues his goals with everything that is within him. London, in his lifetime, would often pursue whatever his latest passion was to the end—sometimes a fruitful end and other times an unsuccessful one. His successful pursuits are well documented. But one example of a failed pursuit is his marriage to Bessie Maddern, in which London pursued his theory of marrying for breeding instead of for love. Another example is his building the *Snark*. His insistence on building it himself led to a barely seaworthy vessel and much unnecessary expense.

In the case of Eden, he pursues his passion until he goes from being an unknown writer to being famous. With fame comes recognition and all the material things he lacked as a starving beginner. Eden struggles with the hypocrisy of the situation. He feels he is still the same—the only thing that has changed is that he has been published.

Unlike Martin Eden, Jack London did not treat his celebrity status as emptiness. Instead, he realized that the money his work demanded could be used to fund his dreams of adventure and his plans for his beloved ranch. He claimed he did not like to write. He once told a friend, "I assure you that I do not write because I love the game. I loathe it. . . . The only reason I write is because I am well paid for my labor—that's what I call it—labor."[3] There may be some truth to these statements, especially when put in perspective with his love of fun and adventure. However, it is obvious he realized that writing was what pulled him from the lower class and that he had indeed succeeded in his work.

# JOHN BARLEYCORN

The second autobiographical work, *John Barleycorn* (1913), was written at Charmian's suggestion. It is subtitled *Alcoholic Memoirs* and describes London's struggle with "John Barleycorn," a nickname at that time for hard liquor. The work focuses solely on London's struggles with alcohol, leaving out many details of his life that would naturally fit in an auto-biography. For example, much of the debauchery likely associated with London's drinking is left out. Many biographers flag him as a womanizer, but none of this is apparent in this work. As a matter of fact, he presents himself as pure emotionally when it comes to women, leaving out the impurity of the physical that is alluded to several times in *Martin Eden*. Once again, the reason for removing the baser parts of the story is because of the editors' sensitivity to their Victorian audiences. This cleanup work actu-ally helps the book, forcing the focus onto London and his ongoing dialogue with John Barleycorn rather than on all the side effects of alcohol.

## OVERVIEW

According to the book, Jack London's first associa-tion with alcohol was at five years old. He was carrying a bucket of beer to his step dad and stopped

This photograph of Jack London and his wife, Charmian, ran as the frontispiece for the 1914 edition of *John Barleycorn*.

to drink some on the way. From this first taste of alcohol, he claimed to hate the taste of the stuff and all drinking after that flowed from it being forced upon him by the demands of society. Of course, it did not help that his stepfather was a drinker and a gambler and took young Jack to the saloons with him. At seven years old, Jack got into a situation where he was given drinks by some Italians. His mother had placed in him a fear of the local Italian immigrants and so he drank drink after drink until he could barely stand. Once at home, he was in bed for days in a delirium. In this delirium, he "wandered deep beneath the ground through a thousand of these dens [of iniquity], and . . . when I would come upon my father, seated at table in these subterranean crypts, gambling with Chinese for great stakes of gold, all my outrage gave vent in the vilest cursing."[4] This delirium proves his close association with saloons even from that early age.

As Jack grew older and began to hang out on the waterfront, he, too, became a regular at the saloons. At first, he drank only when someone bought him drinks. One day, he realized that not only was he expected to accept the drinks of his drinking buddies (which he had done freely for some time), he was supposed to buy a round for everyone. He took this lesson to heart, buying drinks along with everyone else. When he had money, he spent it freely in the bars. London claims that he was called the "Prince of the Oyster Pirates" because of his open hand with his money in the waterfront saloons. As a result of these early experiences, London concludes that to drink is synonymous with manliness, making it a somewhat wholesome form of camaraderie. He reasons, "In the saloons life was different. Men talked with great voices, laughed great laughs, and there was an atmosphere of greatness. Here was something more than common every-day where nothing happened."[5] Even as London moved away from the waterfront and entered into more polite society, he saw the same thing: sharing a drink with another was a way to break down barriers and make fast friends. He used this bit of social etiquette over and over again throughout his life to swap stories or get information.

At one point, London promised Charmian he would stop drinking altogether. After an appalling binge in New York followed by a sober trip around Cape Horn, London decided that social drinking is, in fact, okay, and that he will continue to drink socially, but that alcohol will not master him. He concludes, "No, I decided; I shall take my drink on occasion. . . . I decided coolly and deliberately that I should continue to do what I had been trained to do! I would drink—but, oh, more skillfully, more discreetly, than ever before."[6]

His lowest point came during a period he called the Long Sickness. He felt depressed and defeated. He began having conversations with what he termed the White Logic of his brain. The White Logic held that life was futile, yet it would not release man to death. It longed to live, even if existence meant pain or misery. London, always on the adventure trail, argued for life. It took months before he came out of the Long Sickness. He said that the two things that saved him were socialism and the love of a woman, Charmian. By the end of the book, he finally admits that John Barleycorn has indeed mastered him. All those years of claiming freedom to stop whenever he wanted have led to bondage. He became a heavy drinker and never stopped, even towards the end when he knew that it would shorten his life.

## MERIT AS PROPAGANDA

In the first chapter, London's stated reason for writing the book is that he hoped it would become a Prohibitionist tract. He believed that "[w]hen the women get the ballot, they will vote for prohibition. . . . It is the wives, and sisters, and mothers, and they only, who will drive the nails into the coffin of John Barleycorn."[7] The Prohibition Party, the Young

Christian Temperance Union, and the Women's Temperance Christian Union all promoted the book within their organizations.

This book is another good example of the way London knew his audience and catered to them. Even though the book is all about his drinking lifestyle, in the end he will not change it. He suggests that this book will help those future generations not yet born—both the men and the women who suffer with the men—to avoid the pain that John Barleycorn inflicts. He is unrepentant of his own sins, but he puts forth the hope that his confession will help others with theirs.

# AUTOBIOGRAPHICAL MERIT

London's personification of alcohol as a reasoning being lends an interesting flavor to the book. The struggle seems to be against a force fighting back rather than an inert substance. The amazing thing is the transparency with which London shows his struggles.

Looking back now, almost a hundred years later, London's fight with John Barleycorn shows the typical patterns of an alcoholic's life. Even Charmian, in her diaries, shows the typical response of an alcoholic's partner.[8] London was not the kind of alcoholic who drank himself into oblivion. Instead, he was the social drinker who could not stop. His social life was tied to drink, or at least he perceived it that way. He claimed, "The desire for alcohol is quite peculiarly mental in its origin. It is a matter of mental training and growth, and it is cultivated in social soil."[9] Toward the end of the book he reminisces about how he traveled the world, drink in hand—and that given the chance, he would not change that.

London's insistence in the first three-quarters of the book that he drinks solely for social reasons and that he really doesn't like the taste of it makes his eventual admission that John Barleycorn had defeated him even more potent. "And right there John Barleycorn had me. I was beginning to drink regularly. I was beginning to drink alone."[10] Where once he thought he had control, he lost.

Although modern scholars appreciate London's full body of work, early biographers claimed London's later works were far inferior to his early work. Some attribute it to his increased drinking, others to his demands on himself to simply produce writing to fund his various activities and responsibilities. Either way, he did not reduce his drinking as he grew older. Rather, he increased it. His final realization that he had a problem came at the ranch.

# FARMER
# AND
# FINALE

After their recovery in Australia, London and Charmian returned to California to Beauty Ranch. London's third life change was about to blossom. After experiencing the ravaging diseases and white imperialism of the South Seas, he decided that the closest he would ever get to heaven on earth would be in Sonoma Valley. He found his Eden in his own backyard.[1] He now became a dedicated farmer.

London's primary goal was to apply science to farming for increased yield of crops and best breeding. On his ranch he pioneered in soil conservation, using tillage and terracing to make the worn-out hillside lands fruitful again. He raised vegetables, grains, alfalfa, grapes, fruit trees, prunes, potatoes, spineless cactus, eucalyptus trees, horses, goats, chickens, hogs, beef, dairy cattle, and prize-winning livestock. And he cut the biggest and best hay crops in Sonoma County.[2] Within the first year of his return, in 1910,

London began construction on his dream home, Wolf House.

# "ALL GOLD CANYON"

Several of London's stories from this point on revolve around events in and around Sonoma Valley, with an emphasis on nature as the benevolent source of life. The emphasis switches from man against nature (where nature is the protagonist) to man against nature (where nature is the victim of man's senseless abuse).[3] The earliest example of this theme appears in the short story "All Gold Canyon" (1906), written just after London purchased his first tract of land for Beauty Ranch. The setting is a canyon in the virgin wilderness of California. A miner comes into the canyon, desecrating it in his search for gold. He finds his gold but almost dies when a dark stranger tries to steal it. He kills the stranger instead. Once the miner has what he wants, he continues on, leaving his marks on the canyon. London dramatizes his exit using phrases such as "a ripping and tearing of vines and boughs" and "a clashing of steel-shod hoofs on stone." Once the miner is gone, London uses words like crept, drowsed, whispered, and fluttered to describe the canyon returning back to its peaceful state.

This theme of nature as victim demonstrates a profound shift in London's thinking about nature. Looking at his adventures and the writing that resulted, "his career might well be studied as a life-long series of attempts to escape the corruptions of civilization and to recapture the simple, maternal security of nature."[4] His escape to the wilderness and jungle brought only hardship. His Sonoma Valley stories show that he was close to finding his ideal of nature.

## BURNING DAYLIGHT

This change in attitude toward the environment shows up in three of his novels written after his return from the South Seas. The first, *Burning Daylight* (1910), starts in the Yukon, moves to the city, and then to Sonoma Valley. Burning Daylight is the main character, a man shaped by the rugged environment of the Yukon. He leaves the Northland for San Francisco, where he becomes a successful businessman. He falls in love with his secretary, Dede Mason, and proposes. She refuses him until he finds a new lease on life through escape to the country, emphasizing London's theme of return to the soil for healing restoration.

True to form, London incorporates much of his own experience into this story. Burning Daylight and Dede live on a ranch much like Beauty Ranch, and Dede is much like Charmian. Dede is the driving force behind the success of the ranch. One biographer writes, "The book was . . . a remarkable reaffirmation of Jack's love for Charmian and his optimism about their life in the country."[5]

Critics at the time panned *Burning Daylight*. It seems they never wanted London to leave the Northland. When it was released in 1910, *The New York Times* reported, "The moment [London] steps out of the region where the human animal is pitted against the primal forces of nature in the wilderness, at that moment he loses all grip of the creature and writes of him or her rather more crudely—as to comprehension—than the average schoolboy would."[6] The public was not so disappointed. They liked the love story with a happy ending, buying enough copies of the book to equal one quarter of the total sold for *The Sea-Wolf*.[7]

# TRAGEDY AT HOME

The same year *Burning Daylight* was published, Charmian gave birth to a baby girl. The baby died within hours. Charmian got pregnant again in 1912 but miscarried. She was informed that she would never be able to have children. This ended all hope for an heir for Jack London. He had hoped to pass on his newly acquired property and farming techniques to his sons. This hope highlights yet another departure from socialist thinking.

In 1913 another misfortune occurred. London's dream home, Wolf House, burned down only days before it was ready for occupancy. At the time, the fire was blamed on arson. Many years later it was determined that the fire was actually caused by the combustion of some rags left in the home. The house was not insured and London never tried to rebuild it. He and Charmian continued to live in the same cottage they had occupied since settling on the ranch until his death.

# THE VALLEY OF THE MOON

London wrote two more books featuring locations similar to Beauty Ranch. The first, *The Valley of the Moon* (1913), tells the story of a laundry girl who marries a professional boxer turned teamster. They long to escape from city life and eventually find their Eden in the Valley of the Moon.[8] The story is told in three parts. Book I details the courtship of Saxon and Billy Roberts. London explores their working-class status, emphasizing their hard labor and the callous treatment they receive. Saxon works in a laundry facility, ironing fancy starched clothes for the middle class. Billy works as a teamster, driving horses for a local stable. Book II describes their marriage against the backdrop of union strikes in Oakland, California, where they live. Initially, Billy Roberts exhibits faith in socialism, trusting that the workers' rebellion will break the will of the capitalists. When Billy gets thrown in jail for beating up strike breakers and Saxon has a miscarriage after witnessing violence in the streets, Saxon decides it is time to leave Oakland. Billy agrees to go, his faith in socialism as an agent of change now dead.

**TEAMSTER**—*A person who drives horses for a living.*

Biographers see parts I and II of this book as London's justification for accepting then rejecting the socialist cause. From London's earliest interest in socialism, there were glimpses of disparity between the ideals of socialism and London's writing and lifestyle. In spite of his rugged spirit of individualism, he still believed that socialism was the answer to the evils of capitalism. At first, London believed in a passive approach to building the socialist movement. Later, especially after living in London's East End, he became more of a revolutionary. He eventually resigned from the socialist party, citing their loss of interest in revolution.

Book III documents the travels of Billy and Saxon as they roam the California countryside in search of land for farming. They talk a lot about how their forebears crossed the plains to arrive in California. As they wander, they come across immigrants who have moved to California in more recent years, acquiring land and farming it better than the original immigrants who came across the prairies. Saxon asks lots of questions, studying their methods for producing higher crop yields. They eventually come to Sonoma Valley and find their perfect piece of land. The story ends with Saxon announcing she is pregnant, emphasizing the potential of their new start in life.

The main theme of the novel, escape from the working class into the pastoral dream, closely follows London's own path and desires. Like London, Billy and Saxon Roberts buy land in the Valley of the Moon and farm it using the latest scientific research. Like many of London's heroines, Saxon Roberts is based on Charmian. Saxon embodies the New Woman. It is she who makes the decision to move away from the city and she who advocates scientific farming.

There are a few problems with the novel. The storyline is predictable and the story becomes overburdened with information that does not move the story along. This probably comes from London trying to recount too much of his own life into the novel: his time at Carmel, his positive and negative responses to the immigrants, the details of scientific farming, and so on. In spite of these problems, London manages to work several themes into the novel. One, discussed earlier, is London's justification for becoming a capitalist. The second theme centers on a return to the land, complete with lessons on scientific farming and land conservation. The most poignant theme— and the one most likely to grip his readers—is that of losing faith and finding a new dream.

# THE LITTLE LADY OF THE BIG HOUSE

The last Sonoma Valley book, *The Little Lady of the Big House* (1916), features a love triangle that plays itself out on the large, successful ranch of Dick and Paula Forrest. Dick has poured himself into the running of the ranch, leaving little time for his wife. Paula takes refuge in the arms of Evan Graham, an artistic and sensitive man. When Dick finds out, he makes Paula choose between them. Paula, in love with both of them, chooses suicide to solve the problem.

London often thought his latest book would be completely different than anything else he had written or that was already on the market. This book was no exception. Once again, the critics attacked his work. *The Dial* wrote, "For interesting it certainly is not, after the first few pages."[9] *The Nation* wrote, "He does not achieve reality or sincerity in this performance . . . ."[10] Even modern critics have a hard time finding the good in this novel. The sexual overtones are too stark and the unhappy ending leaves the love triangle unresolved. After this book, London turned away from his agricultural themes. His never-ending pursuit of knowledge led him in new directions.

## THE END OF LIFE

In his last year, 1916, London was plagued by problems but remained excited and energized by new directions in his writing and new philosophies on the horizon. His last stories indicate he was on his way to yet another life change. He was starting to incorporate the ideas of Carl Jung into his writing, evident in his last story, "The Water Baby."

**CARL JUNG**—*Swiss psychiatrist who promoted his ideas on the psychology of the mind. Most noted for his ideas about dream analysis and the collective unconscious.*

During his last few months, London suffered from severe rheumatism and uremia. His kidneys were failing, and nothing short of a radical lifestyle change would help. He spent the first seven months of the year in Hawaii to rest and recover his health. Against his doctors' orders, he never stopped his heavy drinking.

Things at the ranch were going badly, too. His prize stallion died, and he went to trial over water rights on his land. Toward the end, he complained of insomnia. When the inevitable occurred, the doctors' report read:

> At 6:30 P.M., November 21, 1916, Jack London partook of his dinner. He was taken during the night with what was supposed to be an acute attack of indigestion. This, however, proved to be gastrointestinal uraemia. He lapsed into coma and died at 7:45 P.M., November 22.
>
> Dr. W.S. Porter
> Dr. A.M. Thompson
> Dr. W.B. Hays
> Dr. J.W. Shiels[11]

Perhaps London would appreciate the irony of his life, that "after striving so long and so hard to break out from the underworld of the work beast, he succeeded in working himself to death."[12] But he died as he wished—still going strong in pursuing his passions in life.

## POSTHUMOUS PUBLISHING

Because of his work habits and his prolific pen, London had five books ready to publish when he died. They were all published by Macmillan in the next couple of years. Three of these, *The Human Drift*, *Jerry of the Islands*, and *Michael Brother of Jerry* have

**A mural dedicated to Jack London, featuring his famous words: "The proper function of man is to live, not to exist."**

received little attention from scholars. The other two include stories considered to have the depth of his earliest works. *On the Makaloa Mat*, a collection of Hawaiian short stories, includes "The Water Baby," the last story London ever wrote. In it he uses many symbols from Carl Jung's philosophies, showing that he was finally leaving the realm of realism and embracing spirituality.[13] London may have been on the edge of yet another major life change cycle with his renewed interest in spirituality.

**136**

His novella *The Red One* (1918), from the book of the same name, demonstrates that his creative genius was still in full force at the end of his life, as was his continual search for answers and changing philosophy. In this science fiction-like story, a red orb lands in the jungle and becomes a god to the natives. The natives, over generations, have offered human sacrifices to this orb. When struck with a pole, it emits a haunting sound. A scientist visiting the island desires to see what it is that makes this sound. No islander will help him, for they risk death if they reveal its location.

Eventually the scientist catches a fever, but the medicine man of the village will not help him. The medicine man's only desire is to see the scientist die so he can have his head for his devil-devil hut. Dying of the fever, the scientist manages to finagle a way to see what makes the sound. As his dying moment draws near, he feels he has discovered a great mystery that he must share with the world. But this is not to be. Instead, his last vision is of his head twirling slowing in the hut of the medicine man.

The storyline of *The Red One* follows the classic hero outline but falls a couple of steps short of the final stages of the journey. Because the story ends at the moment of enlightenment without going on to resurrection and return, it leaves the piece open to interpretation. Scholars have interpreted it both negatively (where the scientist is disillusioned, focusing on the twirling head), and positively (where the scientist is finally enlightened). It is fitting that at the time London was in the middle of his own search for truth and was, in fact, dying. London had recently read Jung and was exploring the idea of the collective unconscious, represented in this story by the red orb. London died without being able to share what he felt were the revelations of Jung's theories, just as the hero in *The Red One* died before sharing his.

In 1922 Macmillan published *Dutch Courage and Other Stories*. This book is a collection of London's very early stories, with an introduction by Charmian. Still later, in 1963, an unfinished novel, *The Assassination Bureau*, was completed by Robert L. Fish and published by McGraw.

# SUMMARY

London's willingness to bare his soul to his readers, or at least the soul he thought they wanted to read about, endeared him to the public. His life of adventure attracted free spirits and adventurers across the nation. And his willingness to stand up for the underdog endeared him to the common man around the world.

In his day, London was popular and was regularly

in the news for both his writing and his adventures. But as an author, the full body of his work was not fully appreciated until the latter half of the twentieth century. With the perspective of time, there has been a greater appreciation for London's literary talent and his contributions to an understanding of the cultural environment of turn-of-the-century California.

# CHRONOLOGY

**1876**—*January 12:* Jack London born in San Francisco. *September 7:* Flora marries John London.

**1891**—Graduates from grammar school. Holds various jobs, including factory worker (cannery), oyster pirate, and California Fish Patrol.

**1893**—*January–August:* Works aboard the *Sophie Sutherland* as an able-bodied seaman during sealing voyage. *November 12:* Wins first prize in newspaper contest for "Story of a Typhoon Off the Coast of Japan."

**1895**—Returns to high school at age nineteen.

**1896**—Joins Socialist Labor Party. Attends the University of California Berkeley for one semester before dropping out.

**1897**—Begins speaking for socialist causes. *June:* Joins the gold rush to the Klondike. John London dies.

**1898**—*June:* Returns from the Klondike with scurvy. Begins writing career in earnest.

**1899**—Begins publishing short stories in the *Overland Monthly*.

**1900**—*April 7:* Marries Bessie Maddern. First book published, *The Son of the Wolf*, a collection of short stories that appeared in *Overland Monthly*.

**1901**—*January 15:* First daughter, Joan, is born.

**1902**—*July–August:* Spends eight weeks in London's East End researching material for *The People of the Abyss. October 20:* Second daughter, Becky, is born.

**1903**—*The Call of the Wild* is published, catapulting London to worldwide fame. Separates from Bessie Maddern.

**1904**—Travels to Japan and Korea to report on the Russo-Japanese War for Hearst Syndicate. *The Sea-Wolf* is published.

**1905**—*June:* Buys first tract of land for Beauty Ranch near Glen Ellen in Sonoma Valley. *November 19:* Marries Charmian Kittredge.

**1906**—Begins building the *Snark*. Publishes *White Fang*.

**1907**—*April 23:* Sails from San Francisco in the *Snark* with wife Charmian and crew.

**1908**—*The Iron Heel* is published.

**1909**—Abandons *Snark* trip. *Martin Eden* is published.

**1910**—Begins building Wolf House, his dream home. *June 19:* Daughter Joy born; she dies thirty-eight hours after birth. Publishes *Burning Daylight*.

**1912**—Charmian has a miscarriage, ending the couples' hopes of having children. Publishes *The House of Pride*.

**1913**—Wolf House burns down. Publishes *John Barleycorn* and *The Valley of the Moon*.

**1914**—*April:* Reporter for *Collier's* on the Mexican Revolution.

**1915**—Goes to Hawaii to recover health. The *Star Rover* is published.

**1916**—Resigns from Socialist Party. Publishes *The Little Lady of the Big House. November 22:* Dies from gastro-intestinal uremia.

# CHAPTER NOTES

### CHAPTER 1. A MAN OF THE TIMES

1. Alfred Kazin, as quoted in Earle Labor and Jeanne Campbell Reesman, *Twayne's United States Authors Series: Jack London, Revised Edition* (New York: Twayne Publishers, 1994), p. 1.

2. John Perry, *Jack London: An American Myth* (Chicago: Nelson-Hall, 1981), p. 111.

3. Irving Stone, *Jack London: Sailor on Horseback* (New York: Doubleday and Company, 1956), p. 68.

4. Edgar Allen Poe defined a short story as one that could be read in one sitting in his essay "The Philosophy of Composition" in 1846.

5. *The Huntington Library, Art Collections, and Botanical Gardens*, <http://www.huntington.org>. Photocopies of much of London's personal correspondence and his notes can be found on this website.

6. Perry, p. 85.

7. *Twayne's*, p. 38.

8. "Social Darwinism," *Microsoft Encarta Online Encyclopedia*, 2006, <http://encarta.msn.com/encyclopedia_761579584/Social_Darwinism.html> (October 2, 2006).

9. Jack London, "In A Far County," *The Portable Jack London*, Earle Labor, ed. (New York: Penguin Books, 1994), p. 11.

**144**

10. Robert Peluso, "Gazing at Royalty" in *Rereading Jack London*, Leonard Cassuto and Jeanne Campbell Reesman, eds. (Stanford: Stanford University Press, 1996), p. 58.

11. Perry, p. 148.

12. Jack London, *The Sea-Wolf* (New York: Macmillan, 1931), p. 155.

13. Twayne's, p. 38.

## CHAPTER 2. THE MAKING OF A WRITER

1. Irving Stone, *Jack London: Sailor on Horseback* (New York: Doubleday and Company, 1978), p. 31.

2. Jack London, *The Sea-Wolf* (New York: Macmillan, 1931), p. 155.

3. Jack London, "What Life Means to Me," *The Portable Jack London*, Earle Labor, ed. (New York: Penguin Books, 1994), p. 478.

4. Alex Kershaw, *Jack London: A Life* (New York: St. Martin's Press, 1997), p. 66.

5. Franklin Walker, *Jack London & the Klondike* (California: The Huntington Library, 1966), pp. 88–90.

## CHAPTER 3. THE NORTHLAND STORIES

1. Daniel Dyer, *Jack London: A Biography* (New York: Scholastic, Inc., 1997), p. 107.

2. Wolf is the name given to the white man by the Indians of Alaska.

3. Jack London, "The White Silence" in *Jack London: Novels and Stories* (New York: The Library of America, 1958), p. 301.

4. Earle Labor and Jeanne Campbell Reesman,

*Twayne's United States Authors Series: Jack London, Revised Edition* (New York: Twayne Publishers, 1994), p. 26.

5. Jack London. "To Build a Fire" in *Short Stories of Jack London*, Earle Labor, ed. (New York: Macmillan Publishing Company, 1990), p. 283.

6. Ibid., p. 289.

7. Ibid., p. 290.

8. Ibid., p. 295.

9. James Lundquist, *Jack London: Adventures, Ideas, and Fiction* (New York: Continuum, 1990), p. 95.

## CHAPTER 4. A DOG STORY

1. Clarice Stasz, *American Dreamers: Charmian and Jack London* (New York: St. Martin's Press, 1988), p. 110.

2. Jack London, *The Call of the Wild* (New York: Macmillan Publishing Company), 1994, p. 12.

3. Ibid., p. 16.

4. Ibid., p. 46.

5. Ibid., p. 62.

6. Ibid., p. 85.

7. Ibid.

8. Ibid., p. 108.

9. Ibid., p. 116.

10. Ibid., p. 118.

11. James Lundquist, *Jack London: Adventures, Ideas, and Fiction* (New York: Continuum, 1990), p. 107.

12. These stages are based on Joseph Campbell's book *The Hero With a Thousand Faces*.

## CHAPTER 5. BEYOND THE NORTHLAND

1. Jack London, *The Iron Heel*. Footnote in Chapter XVII.

2. Jack London, *The Abyss*, Chapter 24.

3. Jonathan Auerbach, "Congested Mails" in *Rereading Jack London*, Leonard Cassuto and Jeanne Campbell Reesman, eds. (Stanford: Stanford University Press, 1996), p. 37.

4. Alex Kershaw, *Jack London: A Life* (New York: St. Martin's Press, 1997), p. 120.

5. Kershaw, p. 143.

6. John Perry, *Jack London: An American Myth* (Chicago: Nelson-Hall, 1981), p. 281.

## CHAPTER 6. A LOVE STORY

1. Jack London, *The Sea-Wolf and Other Stories* (New York: Penguin Books, 1989), p. 34.

2. Ibid., p. 274.

3. John Perry, *Jack London: An American Myth* (Chicago: Nelson-Hall, 1981), p. 79.

4. Sam S. Baskett, "Sea Change in 'The Sea-Wolf'" in *Rereading Jack London*, Leonard Cassuto and Jeanne Campbell Reesman, eds. (Stanford: Stanford University Press, 1996), p. 108.

5. Earle Labor and Jeanne Campbell Reesman, *Twayne's United States Authors Series: Jack London, Revised Edition* (New York: Twayne Publishers, 1994), p. 60.

## CHAPTER 7. THE OTHER DOG STORY

1. Alex Kershaw, *Jack London: A Life* (New York: St. Martin's Press, 1997), p. 155.

2. Jack London, *White Fang* (New York: Viking, 1999), p. 84.

3. Ibid., p. 109.

4. Ibid., p. 149.

## CHAPTER 8. THE SNARK

1. Jack London, *The Cruise of the Snark* (New York: Sheridan House, 1971, 4th impression 1996), p. 3.

2. London, *The Cruise of the Snark*, p. 339–40.

3. Jack London, "Koolau the Leper" in *The Portable Jack London*, Earle Labor, ed. (New York: Penguin Books, 1994), p. 164.

4. Ibid.

5. James Slagel, "Political Leprosy" in *Rereading Jack London*, Leonard Cassuto and Jeanne Campbell Reesman, eds. (Stanford: Stanford University Press, 1996), p. 185.

6. Jack London, *South Seas Tales* (New York: Dover Publications, 2001), pp. 47–8.

7. Earle Labor and Jeanne Campbell Reesman, *Twayne's United States Authors Series: Jack London, Revised Edition* (New York: Twayne Publishers, 1994), p. 92.

## CHAPTER 9. SEMI-AUTOBIOGRAPHICAL NOVELS

1. Jack London, *John Barleycorn or, Alcoholic Memoirs* (New York: Penguin Group, 1990), p. 126.

2. Jack London, *Martin Eden* (New York: Penguin Books, 1993), p. 482.

3. John Perry, *Jack London: An American Myth* (Chicago: Nelson-Hall, 1981), p. 296.

4. London, *John Barleycorn*, p. 32.

5. Ibid., p. 38.

6. Ibid., p. 236–237.

7. Ibid., p. 15.

8. Clarice Stasz, *American Dreamers: Charmian*

*and Jack London* (New York: St. Martin's Press, 1988), pp. 231–232.

9. London, *John Barleycorn*, pp. 234–235.

10. Ibid., pp. 190–191.

## CHAPTER 10. FARMER AND FINALE

1. Earle Labor and Jeanne Campbell Reesman, *Twayne's United States Authors Series: Jack London, Revised Edition* (New York: Twayne Publishers, 1994), p. 92.

2. Jack London's Beauty Ranch, "Jack London the Visionary." <http://www.jacklondons.net/intro.html> (December 22, 2005).

3. *Twayne's*, p. 96.

4. *Twayne's*, p. 84.

5. Clarice Stasz, *American Dreamers: Charmian and Jack London* (New York: St. Martin's Press, 1988), p. 198.

6. *New York Times*, November 5, 1910, as quoted in John Perry, *Jack London: An American Myth* (Chicago: Nelson-Hall, 1981), p. 246.

7. Alex Kershaw, *Jack London: A Life* (New York: St. Martin's Press, 1997, p. 225.

8. The Valley of the Moon is the American Indian name for Sonoma Valley, California.

9. John Perry, *Jack London: An American Myth* (Chicago: Nelson-Hall, 1981), p. 297.

10. Ibid.

11. *San Francisco Chronicle*, November 23, 1916, as published in Perry, p. 300.

12. *Twayne's*, p. 82.

13. Ibid., pp. 128–129.

# GLOSSARY

**agrarian**—Relating to the land or agriculture.

**androgyny**—A blending of both male and female characteristics.

**Bildungsroman**—A novel dealing with the education or development of a young protagonist, who then takes his place in society as a mature or knowledgeable adult.

**capitalism**—An economic system where the means of production and distribution are privately owned and operated.

**Darwinism**—Theory of evolution through natural selection popularized by Charles Darwin in his book *Origin of the Species.*

**determinism**—The belief that every idea and action is predetermined and cannot be changed; negating a person's free will.

**Golden Age of Magazines**—The period in American history when magazine production was at its highest due to new technologies of the Industrial Age.

**Hearst Syndicate**—Newspaper operation owned by William Randolph Hearst.

**hero cycle**—A process of personal growth in which the person goes through several stages that require change. They are a call to adventure, departure, initiation, transformation, and return. The end result is a return to the point of origin with new information or new skills to benefit others.

**hyperbole**—Bold overstatement for ironic or comic effect.

**idealist**—One who follows ideals rather than practical considerations.

**imperialists**—Those who support the extension of a nation's rule over foreign countries by exercise of political or economic authority.

**individualism**—Elevating self-reliance of the individual over society as a whole.

**Industrial Age**—The period of rapid industrialization in America from about 1850 until the early 1900s, beginning with the expansion of travel and product distribution through steam locomotives and steam engines on ships and culminating with the invention of electricity. Factories proliferated, producing goods for mass consumption.

**irony**—The use of words to express an idea or ideas that are the opposite of the words' literal meaning.

**Klondike**—A region of Canada along the Klondike River, just east of Alaska.

**leprosy**—A chronic disease of the skin, flesh, and nerves resulting in ulcers, scaly skin, and deformities caused by nerve damage.

**Materialist**—One who believes that the physical world is the only reality, and all things can be explained in those terms.

**Naturalism**—A style of fiction in which a character's life is determined strictly by his surroundings and genetics. The individual does not have a spirit but lives completely within the physical realm of nature.

**Nature Fakir**—Those who falsify the natural world in order to make a point or further an agenda.

**primordial**—Being primary, or happening first, in time.

**Prohibition**—Law forbidding the manufacture or sale of liquor and other alcoholic beverages.

**protagonist**—The main character in a novel or other piece of writing.

**schism**—A division with opposing sides.

**scurvy**—A disease caused by a vitamin C deficiency, resulting in anemia, swollen gums, and weakness.

**serialization**—Publishing a story in parts at regular intervals. Magazines often serialized novels by printing a new chapter in each issue.

**short story**—Fictional narrative prose that focuses on a single incident or a very short period of time.

**Social Darwinism**—The application of Darwin's theory of evolution through natural selection to human social institutions. Popularized by Herbert Spencer.

**socialism**—An economic system in which the means of production and distribution are owned and operated by the government with all members of society sharing in the work and the products.

**suffrage**—The right to vote.

**teamster**—A person who drives horses for a living.

**uremia**—A toxic condition that occurs when the body does not properly eliminate waste products in the urine.

**Victorian Age**—The time of Queen Victoria's reign over the United Kingdom (1837–1901). In general, novels of that time period were stories of romance in which the woman sought the perfect domestic life with the perfect man. The stories often included moral lessons of right and wrong, with appropriate justice administered to each class of character.

**yellow peril**—In late 1800s, the fear that Chinese and Japanese immigration would lower the value of the American worker. The phrase was used prominently in newspapers in the Hearst Syndicate.

# MAJOR WORKS BY JACK LONDON

"Story of a Typhoon Off the Coast of Japan" (1893)

*The Son of the Wolf* (1900)

*The God of His Fathers* (1901)

*Children of the Frost* (1902)

*A Daughter of the Snows* (1902)

*The Kempton–Wace Letters* (1903)

*The Call of the Wild* (1903)

*The People of the Abyss* (1903)

*The Sea-Wolf* (1904)

*Tales of the Fish Patrol* (1905)

*Moon-Face and Other Stories* (1906)

*White Fang* (1906)

*The Road* (1907)

*The Iron Heel* (1908)

*Martin Eden* (1909)

*Lost Face* (1910)

*Burning Daylight* (1910)

*Revolution and Other Essays* (1910)

*When God Laughs and Other Stories* (1911)

*The Cruise of the Snark* (1911)

*South Sea Tales* (1911)

*The House of Pride and Other Tales of Hawaii* (1912)

*The Night Born* (1913)

*John Barleycorn* (1913)

*The Valley of the Moon* (1913)

*The Scarlet Plague* (1915)

*The Star Rover* (1915)

*The Little Lady of the Big House* (1916)

*The Red One* (1918)

*On the Makaloa Mat* (1919)

*Jack London Reports* (1979)

# FURTHER READING

Bankston, John. *Jack London*. Bear, Del.: Mitchell Lane, 2004.

Bloom, Harold, ed. *Jack London*. Broomall, Pa.: Chelsea House, 2001.

Kershaw, Alex. *Jack London: A Life*. New York: St. Martin's Press, 1999.

Stefoff, Rebecca. *Jack London: An American Original.* New York: Oxford University Press, 2002.

# INTERNET ADDRESSES

**The Jack London Collection**
http://london.centenary.edu/main.html

**The Jack London Papers at the Huntington Library**
http://www.huntington.org/LibraryDiv/jlpapers.html

**Jack London State Historic Park**
http://www.parks.sonoma.net/JLPark.html

# INDEX

## A

adventures, 32, 35, 38, 74, 102
Alger, Horatio, 29, 47
Anglo-Saxon superiority, 20, 48, 110
anthropomorphism, 24, 70
autobiographical works, 113–125

## B

Beauty Ranch, 15, 47, 81, 102, 103, 112, 118, 125, 126–128, 129, 130, 135, 141
Bildungsroman, 115, 116, 149
Brett, George, 55–56, 73, 76, 83, 92
*Burning Daylight*, 128–129, 141

## C

*Call of the Wild, The*, 5, 7, 19, 21, 24, 54, 55–72, 73, 76, 90, 91, 92, 99–100, 141
capitalism, 35, 131, 149
children, 129, 141, 142
class issues, 9, 21, 25, 31, 36, 47, 75, 79–80, 106, 113–118, 130–132

## D

Darwin, Charles, 19, 37, 66, 72, 84, 149, 152
Darwinism, 19, 37, 87, 149
death, 135
determinism, 67–68, 96–97, 100, 149
divorce, 81–82, 91

## G

gender, 22, 89, 132, 134
Golden Age of Magazines, 11, 149

## H

Hawaii, 17, 20, 32, 101, 103–109, 112, 134, 142
health problems, 40, 81, 105, 110, 126, 134, 135, 140, 142
hero cycle, 56, 71–72, 137–138

## I

imperialism, 17, 20, 109, 126
Industrial Age, 9, 27, 34, 150
*Iron Heel , The,* 10, 112, 141
irony, 23, 110–111, 135, 150

**J**

*John Barleycorn*, 113, 119–125

Jung, Carl, 134, 136, 138

**K**

*Kempton-Wace Letters, The*, 76–77, 81, 82, 154

Klondike, 8, 17, 19, 20, 23, 38, 40–41, 46, 48, 49, 50, 53, 81, 94, 140

"Koolau the Leper," 106–108

**L**

Larsen, Wolf, 83–90

life changes, 8, 32, 33, 36, 41, 117–118, 126

London, Charmian, 22, 82, 89, 91, 105–106, 119, 120, 122–124, 126, 129, 130, 132, 138, 14, 142

London, Eliza, 27, 38

Long Sickness, The, 123

**M**

MacMillan, 55, 73, 92, 138

Maddern, Bessie, 43, 47, 76, 77, 81–82, 90, 117, 140, 141

Malemute Kid, 24, 42, 43, 44–45

marriages, 43, 54, 73, 76–7, 82, 91, 117, 140, 141

*Martin Eden*, 15, 22, 37, 112, 113–118, 119, 141

Marx, Karl, 9–10, 36

"Mauki," 110–111

Mexican Revolution, 80, 142

**N**

Naturalism, 18–19, 23, 43–44, 66, 69, 96, 100, 128, 151

Nature Fakir, 100, 151

New Woman, 22, 89, 132

Nietzsche, Frederich, 87

**O**

Oakland Free Library, 29, 36

**P**

*People of the Abyss, The*, 74–75, 79, 141

posthumous publishing, 135–138

prohibition, 16, 17, 123, 151

**R**

race issues, 17, 20, 23, 77, 79, 87, 108, 109, 110, 126

Roosevelt, Theodore, 12, 13, 17, 78, 100–101

Russo-Japanese War, 77–80

## S

San Francisco, 14, 26, 31, 32, 33, 38, 54, 83, 103, 105, 128, 140, 141, 148

scientific farming, 126–127

*Sea-Wolf, The*, 21, 22, 33, 72, 82–91, 129, 141

serialization, 11, 13, 55, 151, 152

*Snark*, 101, 102–105, 107–111, 118, 141

Social Darwinism, 20, 37, 48, 143, 152

socialism, 8, 10, 16, 35, 36, 74, 81, 91, 123, 131, 152

socialist, 8, 10, 35, 37, 47, 73, 74–75, 79–81, 112, 114, 117, 130, 131, 140, 142

Sonoma Valley, 126, 127–128, 132–133, 148

*Sophie Sutherland*, 32–33, 83, 140

Spencer, Herbert, 37, 66, 152

Sterling, George, 15, 117

Strunsky, Anna, 76–77, 81–82

## T

"The Red One," 137–138

"The Water Baby," 134, 136

"To Build a Fire," 48–53

"To the Man on Trail," 42, 43, 44

## U

understanding of market, 13, 17, 47, 56, 70–71, 109, 133, 138

## V

*Valley of the Moon, The*, 75, 130–133, 142, 148

Victorian Age, 12, 152

Victorian audience, 21, 22, 25, 85, 88, 119

## W

*White Fang*, 19, 21, 24, 90, 91, 92–101, 141

White Silence, 23, 24, 41, 44–45, 52

Wolf House, 127, 130, 141, 142

## Y

yellow peril, 79, 153